WEST SIDE STORIES

NOTES FROM NORTHOLT

STUART DEABILL

Stuart Deabill (signature)

SOUL
DEEP

Published in Great Britain in 2021 by Soul Deep Productions
Printed and bound in Great Britain by Clays Ltd, Elcograf S.p.A..
ISBN 978-1-7397586-0-8

MIX
Paper from
responsible sources
FSC® C018072

www.souldeep.co.uk

Dedicated to my mum, dad, sister and the Wood End kids.
May you all shine on.

Contents

Foreward

The phrase 'university of life' is often overused and has become somewhat of a cliché, but I must be honest and say that this is what I was mainly thinking as I made my way through this very entertaining book.

To me, it is the story of there being no career path or plan, and no further education being tacked on, after school had been finished with. In truth, that was nothing to be surprised by. It was standard of the era and background detailed here. The majority of teachers had missed the natural intelligence that was on show, but that was OK; it would simply be channelled outside of those academic constraints they lived by. By the time school was done, a variety of items, be they tickets, or trainers had been bought and sold, so the knowledge was there that spotting an opportunity and making some gelt from it was doable. This was the thrill of the chase, where a fiver became a tenner, and was used as supplementary income to then fuel the excess energy running through the body.

Just one undemanding nine to five job, was never going to be enough. Too many ideas were spinning around the 'never off duty' swede. Fingers were going in pies. Some were hot, and yes, some cold. After all, no one gets a coconut every time.

Over the years, I guess Stuart's activities would see him described as a sort of Del Boy or Arthur Daley, with him described as 'ducking and diving.' To me however, that is a lazy phrase, though I will concede there were elements of that on show here.

No, this life was not fiction, this life was lived in a world of fact. Natural instincts were honed from many nights spent in edgy pubs and clubs, when at any moment it could all go bandy around you. Of course, you would stand and fight if needs be, but you'd be away on your toes, with the goods that you were trying to sell still in your possession or, even sweeter, be clean away, holding the folding you had made from that night's graft.

Notes From Northolt is full of stories that will make you smile, laugh, or simply shake your head in wonder. I'll wager one or two reading this book, will have had similar experiences and tales to tell. However, the impressive difference here is your author has a forensic memory to lean on, and story-telling skills would have gone down a storm round a campfire in the old days, or a pub table nowadays.

A page-turner awaits you.

Mark Baxter, Summer 2021

Introduction

I've had the idea for a biographical book floating around for many years. I'd started writing pieces (with a pen!) some 20 years ago but it's only been the last ten years or so, since buying a PC and using social media, that I've had the confidence to put articles out on the music and culture I love. A blog helped me shape a story, even if my grammar was primary school level. However, people seemed to like what I was writing, and it got me some attention. When I was asked to co-write a book on London clubland with Ian Snowball in 2011, shit got real. And, with varying degrees of success following books on my favourite band, The Jam, and *the* group of the 90s, Oasis, the love and respect shown was enough to make me think I might be alright at this. Then a job as a copywriter, creating website content for businesses and getting the respective companies on Page 1 of Google, improved my grammar dramatically. And with help from my boss and friend Paul Miceli, he taught me how to hone my craft.

I got sacked from the job after a couple of years because, as much as I tried, I just couldn't make a mechanic in Lytham St Annes sound sexy. And I was more interested in posting on Facebook than writing about how to remove Japanese knotweed from a garden in Basildon.

So, *Notes From Northolt* stayed a short collection of half-finished observations due to either work schedules, being on the road with the band I managed, or a fear of my stories being accepted or bought outside of friends and family. I mean, I'm not 'a name', and I'm not desperate to be famous or in the public eye. Well, not since I turned 50 anyway. But after publisher-turned-agent Chris Newson encouraged me to finish the project and wanted to represent me because he thought I had a talent for storytelling, I was determined to get to the end of it. He also thought I should stop at the end of the millennium, to give the book a youthful rite-of-passage tone, plus I moved out of Northolt in 2001 so it wouldn't have made much sense being called *Notes From Northolt* and being about shit that happened whilst living in Dunstable or Watford.

For those who don't know, Northolt is a suburban town 11 miles west of London and is famous for its RAF base. But for me, and most of my mates who grew up there, it's more about the spirit of the place and the friendships forged through its schools, parks and pubs. Northolt is stamped right through me, and it'll continue to be until I draw my last. Don't take life too seriously. Earn a couple of quid. Have each other's back.

What drove me to start writing my memoirs is my undiluted passion for music, football, the 'look' and the many avenues they've taken me down. I love good television and film as well, but it's the 'Holy Trinity' that fully captures my imagination. It's a lifestyle many working-class fellas have followed, including a good percentage of my pals. And, as any of them will tell you, it's never just been about what happens on the pitch or on a stage, but the stuff that happens around a game or gig too. I've also included stories of work and other misdemeanours that have crossed my path.

I also take in some of the events of my early years, from following bands to playing in them. Kickabouts in the park to full-scale riots in continental stadia. Devouring *Minder* on the telly to emulating the bold Arfur's traits. From purchasing Sergio Tacchini tracksuits from Stuarts in Shepherds

Bush to selling knock-off Stone Island Jumpers out of the back of a Ford Escort in Greenford. From buying the books and records of my heroes to becoming mates with them and other trade-offs. You'll soon get snapshots of the golden paths I've glided down and the icy roads I've crashed on.

Each chapter or entry is a short story of a time, place and a piece of my own personal history, told to the best of my knowledge or, at least, how I remembered it. The good, the bad and the ridiculous. There's a good possibility *Notes* will trigger personal memories and remind you of certain circumstances or scenarios you've experienced along the way. I hope you laugh along, like I've laughed out loud at some of the things I've reminded myself about, especially the stories buried deep in my psyche for the best part of 40-odd years. I can honestly say that I was lucky to experience so much in those carefree pre-millennium days and to be given the freedom to do it all. Well, to be honest, no-one could have stopped me. My fear of missing out was at OCD level.

Because I was the one who usually organised tickets, transport and hotels, it meant that I always had good company on every trip. Without larging it, I think I've been blessed with good taste in music and clobber. Well, most of the time. So, once those early punk records set my course, I became obsessed with what influenced the artists. I was always reaching back to check the links. Soul music was all around me through constantly hearing Motown and STAX records at parties growing up. That's the root of it all. And I can't overstate the importance of the radio. It's been on in every house I've ever lived in and every job I've ever had. I've been a delivery driver or out on the road doing other things, so I've heard everything current, good and bad, day and most evenings, especially in the days before DAB. (My knowledge held me in good stead on Radio 2's *Popmaster* some years back. 36 points and a Cuddly Ken Radio. Bosh.)

I read Smash Hits magazine every other week before it was time to grow up, be a man and take the *NME* to my heart. And I didn't miss an issue of that for 20 years. Stick *Melody Maker, Record Mirror* and *Mojo* in there. It just made sure I didn't miss the next big thing.

By 1990, all the guitars and rock were thrown to one side as I was fully immersed in the club/house scene, and so started a whole new strand of record collecting. I suppose there was a nerd element about it all, but I was never one of those snotty cunts who kept it to himself.

"Al! You should hear this!"

"Simon! Let's go and see them!"

"Sean! Let's get tickets for so and so!"

However, by 1994 I was growing bored with weekend clubbing and getting so ruined that I didn't feel right till Wednesday, so when Oasis happened, it felt like the time was right to change tack.

Football. Chelsea, the religion. Their results used to affect my moods and I was very moody in the early 80s! During those times, me and my pal, Lock who lived up on Dorchester Road, used to go to most games and a few away. History tells us we watched the worst Chelsea side ever, one that flirted dangerously with the old Third Division and the possibility of extinction. Chairman Ken Bates turned things round in the summer of 1983, and a team to love, to follow and to fight for got promoted the following season! And some 40 years on, we still sit together. Win or lose, Up the Blues!

During the 90s, that all changed as I started meeting more like-minded chaps and, sometimes, struggled to get out of the pub for a match. Same with the aggro once it started to become more and more honed. It made sense going to away games with faces so that I wasn't picked out for wearing Stone Island or CP Company outerwear. Amazing how a brand or look can define you. My thing was always about getting to see the game. I never wanted to miss a game because Leicester's Baby Squad had called it on at 3.30 in a deserted park. I left all that for those on a ban or the loons who loved fighting. And there were plenty of them.

Music, football and clobber. The defining trinity that forged the loyal friendships and gave me an escape from the humdrum. It was my life, and do you know what? It's still my foundation.

Stuart Deabill, 2021

Roots and Echoes

Northolt was pretty much farmland and fields, a quiet outpost on the west London Borough of Ealing until the 1930s when the A40 trunk road was built with mass housing to serve the ever-growing population of London. The fact it was a supposedly a former Saxon/Viking settlement explains a lot. There's always been a touch of rebel about the area.

As the Second World War raged, Northolt became a key area. Its RAF base, the oldest in the UK, played a major part in the Battle of Britain. It became the home of Hurricane and Spitfire planes. Several units, including the Polish Fighter Squadron, engaged the Germans whilst they attacked and bombed London. The Polish War Memorial on the junction of Western Avenue and West End Road is a fitting monument to their bravery, even if it's now more famous for being a traffic hot spot, as many West Londoners will testify.

In the 1950s and 60s, families were moved from slum clearances and compulsory purchased homes in the Notting Hill and Notting Dale areas to make way for the Westway, the elevated stretch of road connecting London to suburbs of the west. They ended up on newly built council estates such as the Racecourse, Islip Manor and White Hart. Also, housing was cheap to buy in the area and was served by two stations, one underground and one overground, with easy access into Central London. The A40 splits the town and I always joked that living to the East of Northolt, in the Wood End area where I grew up, meant we were from the posh side.

A bit like comparing Lidl to Aldi.

I can't honestly say that if I'd have been brought up anywhere else, I wouldn't have had the same drive or spirit, but I'm pretty sure my life would have been less interesting. Northolt was a solid place to get pissed, get high, play up, plot dreams, schemes and ideals, and live life to the full. No-one felt rooted to the spot either. A lot of my mates wouldn't think twice about travelling the world in search of the craic, usually while on the dole. From Amsterdam to Goa, from San Francisco to Bangkok, and from Manchester to Magaluf, be it football, thieving, partying, whoring or sometimes all four. And, wherever possible, bunking the fare.

To pay is to fail.

The 80s was a fantastic decade for taking liberties, long before the onset of CCTV, everything was cash. Before drugs took hold in the 90s, the local pubs were a good place to buy and receive stolen goods. I remember one Friday night in my local pub The Swan, where a local fence had everything from Panasonic VHS recorders to Eric Clapton CDs, from Cabbage Patch dolls to rabbits for sale, all from the back of his Ford Sierra. Northolt always knew how to have it large. Too much so at times, but it was never boring.

Route 66

I was born in St Mary Abbot's Hospital, in West Kensington, on Tuesday 9th August, 1966. I've no idea what time I made my entrance, but I assume it was early as I've not been able to sleep in for many years. Carpe diem and all that. Being born into a city that I've long considered the best in the world, with what I hope was an amazing afterglow of England's only World Cup win, still feels slightly special. It also makes me one of the oldest bods who hadn't been around to see Bobby Moore lift the Jules Rimet Trophy, and I've never really liked missing out on a party.

My mum, Val, and my dad, Derek, met while working at the General Post Office in 1959. Dad was a telephone engineer based at South Kensington exchange and Mum was a telephonist putting calls through the system. After a blind date that went hopelessly wrong, my mum relented to a second date and the rest is history. They got married in Twickenham in 1963 and moved in with my dad's folks, Violet and Fred, at 14 Faroe Road in West Kensington.

Dad was born in London in September 1939, so all his early memories are of war. There was talk of evacuation, but my nan was a fearless character. There'd be no talk of her giving over her only child to some "cross-eyed farmer's family".

Del remembers waking up after yet another night in the garden bomb shelter, walking to school after a bombing raid, and seeing the house down the end of the road reduced to rubble. My grandad was in the RAF and although he told every one of my mates that he was a Spitfire

16

pilot, Fred was one of the ground staff at RAF Lyneham. Grandad said there was nothing sadder than fewer planes coming back to base than going out at the start of the day.

Mum was born in October 1941 in Edinburgh, where Grandad Norman and Grandma Marjorie were stationed. Norman was in the Royal Dragoons, so they moved about a bit, including a stint in Germany straight after the end of the war, before settling in Twickenham, in south-west London, with her brothers Geoff, Tony and Peter.

My memories of living at Faroe Road are pretty much non-existent. My mum and dad moved out in 1968 but I somehow knew it had an outside shithouse before I asked the old man about it recently. Funny innit how every autobiography of a working-class musician, actor or footballer, born before me, always mentions how their house had an outside toilet like it's some badge of honour. How they struggled before they hit the big time and all that bollocks.

"We were so poor, the urine would freeze on exit when we took a piss" or "Every Sunday, the whole family used to have a bath in front of the coal fire listening to *Family Favourites* on the wireless. There'd be me, my sister, my brother and Tonto the Jack Russell in there together, just to save on hot water".

There was an inside toilet too but, when my nan bought the house in the early 1950s for less than the owner wanted, but he couldn't face old Violet driving him mad on the cost, the tight bastard went and removed the toilet before he handed over the keys. The cost of 14 Faroe Road back then? £1200. The current value in 2021? £1.2 million. Once the likes of me leave London, you leave for good.

Go West

188 Wood End Lane, a two-bedroom house in Northolt, opposite a Threshers off-licence and a general store or, as we called it, 'The Paper Shop'. Dad was still with the GPO. Mum was a housewife, soon to become a hairdresser.

I can't honestly remember what my first memory is, which makes me sound like I've already got the onset of Alzheimer's, but I did pick up reading quickly.

The *Daily Mirror TV Guide*, I'm reliably told, was my first foray into my love of the written word just so I could see what was on *Watch with Mother*.

Watch with Mother was the first dedicated pre-school kids TV sequence to hit the ever-growing number of TV screens in 1953, with programmes such as *Andy Pandy* and *The Woodentops*. First broadcast between 3.45pm and 4pm, it was timed to hit kids after a post-afternoon nap, and before the older brothers or sisters came home from school and destroyed the relative peace. All primitive stuff.

By 1968, many homes had a TV, and most children were au fait with the likes of *Camberwick Green* and *Pogles Wood*. There's me, aged two-and-a-half, desperate to see if favourites such as the cartoon, *Mary, Mungo and Midge* or the puppet show, *The Herbs*, was on.

Mary had a dog (Mungo) and a mouse (Midge). She lived in a tower block. It was probably the first time urban living had been featured in a cartoon. Later on, a geezer who I worked with at the Post-Office lived in Gleneagles Tower, a block on the Golf Links Estate in Southall. He kept a python, a hamster, a couple of parakeets and a lizard in his two-bed flat. Back in the 70s and 80s, having your own mini-zoo 17 floors up wasn't that uncommon!

Tower blocks were a new phenomenon at the time, with planners heralding high-rise living as the future. Then the authorities let most of them fall into disrepair and, tragically and famously, led to the deaths of 72 occupants when nearby Grenfell Tower caught fire in 2017. The planners' dream went well wrong.

The Herbs had an array of characters such as Parsley the Lion, Dill the Dog and, my favourite, Sir Basil. Monocled up and wearing a deerstalker hat (which became the headwear of choice for some of the chaps at football some years later), Basil was into hunting and fishing but wasn't very good at either. His wife, Lady Rosemary, used to keep Basil under the thumb. She was very prim, and pretty much like every woman over the age of 60 living in Pinner, Tring or Chalfont St Giles.

Mum and Dad both loved music, but especially Dad. He was a big Jazz fan and saw all the greats, from Count Basie and Miles Davis to homegrown legends such as Tubby Hayes and Georgie Fame. And, of course, that love for going against the grain rather than sticking to the conformity of the pop charts or daytime radio seeped into my consciousness.

However, the first song that made an impression was a cheeky call-

and-response record that reached Number 1 in 1968 by Esther & Abi Ofarim titled *Cinderella Rockafella*. I was only reminded of this when Mum sent me a copy of the 7" for my 52nd birthday. I looked at it and didn't recognise the artist or place any connection to the title. It was only when I stuck it on the turntable that it all came flooding back. A ragtime love song that had me transfixed. A bit strange, but catchy as fuck. My Grandma was constantly told "again", by an excited me, to keep playing the record repeatedly at her home in Bourne End, Buckinghamshire, always with my family encouraging me to show off.

I can only imagine the shapes I was pulling.

Mind you, this was mild compared to my love of 'Lily the Pink', which was released the following year by the scouse trio, Scaffold. The line-up included Paul McCartney's brother, Mike, a fantastic poet in Roger McGough, and the lunatic John Gorman who was better known to my generation a decade later in the best kids' TV show ever, *Tiswas*. That was the first record I ever owned. God help my poor parents having to listen to it 48 times a day.

Mum was more radio friendly and, even though she wasn't a record buyer as such, she loved the big vocals of Dusty Springfield and Bobbie Gentry. The radio was always on in the kitchen and Ed Stewart's Junior Choice, and the brilliant Johnny Walker (who I still religiously listen to on a Sunday) took precedence over the old man moaning about work or digging out the neighbour whose house backed onto us, his weekly bonfire inevitably stinking our gaff out.

"What's he burning now? Bleedin' horse muck? What's up with him? Every bloody week!" and so forth.

In March 1970, we were joined by my only sibling. My sister, Nicole, was born in Perivale Maternity Hospital, which was nice.
That's the family. All good in the hood.

Around this time, I started nursery and moved on to Wood End Infant School for my first taste of formal education. In my class was my oldest mate, Greg Phillips. Greg was obsessed with football and that opened a whole new world to me. Kicking a ball about, jumpers for goalposts, 15-a-side. The beautiful game in its purest and rawest form.
Obsessed!

Greg's dad, Peter, was a semi-professional and had played non-league, and for clubs in South Africa, and had obviously passed down his passion and drive for the game to Greg and his younger brother, Martin. The Phillips family were staunch Chelsea. Chelsea FC had just won the European Cup Winners' Cup and were one of the glamour sides of the Football League. Players like Peter Osgood, Charlie Cooke and Alan Hudson oozed class, confidence and success.

Some of Greg's family had season tickets and used to take him along, even at that age. Greg was a cool cat and told me to support them, so I did. Every breaktime was spent playing football. My talking Action Man had a Chelsea tracksuit and I'd watch ITV's The Big Match religiously every Sunday. Sounds a bit weird now, dressing up a man doll, but I think once the old man stopped him from speaking by stepping on it with bare feet, it soon got fucked off for the Striker game and, later, Johnny Hot Shot (Ask your weird uncle, kids.)

The élan of the early 70s had waned rapidly, and Chelsea were forced to have a massive overhaul, partly due to player power, but also because of lack of funds thanks to the cost of the new East Stand, which is now the oldest part of Stamford Bridge. Dramatically, in May 1975, Chelsea was relegated to the 2nd Division by their fiercest rivals, Tottenham Hotspur. My Dad liked football and supported QPR as they were his local team, but he wasn't much of a match-goer. I think he preferred the races or the dogs, much like Grandad Fred. However, we did go to some games and my first was QPR vs Manchester City at Loftus Road, which was Rodney Marsh's first game back after leaving the Rangers. My Dad got tickets right at the back of the South Africa Stand so I could stand up and watch the game unhindered without pissing anyone off. I did ask him to take me to Chelsea, but I was always met with "Sorry son. It's too violent." One of his workmates would get me a programme though, so I had some connection, however tenuous.

Liverpool, the team of the day, were exciting to watch and, in Kevin Keegan, had an exciting striker who lit up the pitch. He certainly became my favourite player around that time, especially when playing for England. As most of a certain age know, there was very little live football on television back then. England games and FA Cup Finals were pretty much it. At 8 years old, I was yet to realise pure football tribalism and the downside of those loveable scousers. My Dad somehow get tickets for the

1978 European Cup Final, when Liverpool beat Bruges 1-0 at Wembley. That was my first visit to the old stadium, and I have vivid memories of my first glimpse of that glorious pitch and its lush green carpet, as well as the smell of beer and geezers pissing where they stood. I avoided a 'hot leg', but I don't know if the old man was as lucky. It does mean that I've still seen Liverpool win the European Cup more times than most of their 'fans'!

The only thing that held me back in those pre-teen days and knocked my confidence was being born with a cyst in my eye. A semi-circular milky looking thing. I stood out a bit, and it got me some stick.
"Oi! Rice Crispie Eye! Milky!"

By the time I'd negotiated infant school, Dad found a bigger house for sale round the corner in Killowen Avenue and, in 1974, we moved to number 38, where me and my sister got our own bedrooms. I started junior school that autumn at the newly christened Greenwood and had to wear a green blazer. The rival junior school, Wood End, which was attached to Greenwood who wore grey and were literally at the other end of our school, royally took the piss out of this and we were known as Green Bogeys. Oh, the banter.

Academically, I picked up reading to a good degree and just cracked on. Highlights of the school year would have been our sports day, days out to places like The Commonwealth Institute and, again, playing football morning, noon and night. I struggled to get into the school team though. Greg was the captain and had become a David Watts (see

The Kinks or The Jam for reference) type of character. I made the odd substitute appearance.

It was in junior school where Graham, a lad in my class had become a bit of a bullying bastard and would dig out certain kids, including myself. I didn't like this special attention and avoided him wherever possible; difficult in a classroom when he's saying he's going to get you after the lesson and he's sitting by the door!

I wasn't much of a fighter, so I was put on my arse more than once and usually stayed there. Bullying is the ultimate cunt's trick but, at eight or nine, how can you deal with that? And nobody likes a grass. Teachers certainly wouldn't have recognised it in the same way they do now. Most of them wanted to get home as quickly as we did, without much fuss. His mum had died and although I get it now, it wasn't my fucking fault, was it?

It came to a head when my jacket in the cloakroom was left in a corner covered in piss. Mrs Mortimer, the fat charmless nurse, called my mum and told her my jacket had been urinated on, and asked her to bring a new one for me to wear on the way home. Obviously, Mum was upset, and Dad was livid. Dad was chairman of the PTA, so it must have been even harder to deal with.

I'm not sure what happened afterwards with the respective parents, but the bullying seemed to subside, partly due to an operation I'd had to remove the cyst out of my left eye. I was off school for a long time. The op was in June 77 at the height of the Jubilee and of course The Sex Pistols, and the subsequent school holiday coincided. Even though Graham still growled every now and then on return, I sort of ignored it as the gripping spell of fear and getting hurt diminished.

Early lesson learnt.

Stamford Bridge

Aged 13, I finally got to go to a Chelsea game. It was a big one as the team were pushing for promotion back to Division 1. It was also Ron 'Chopper' Harris's last game after spending his whole footballing career with The Blues. The old man finally relented after I asked if I could go with Greg and his brother Martin and, more importantly, his dad. I used Greg's old boy as a foil for the next couple of seasons whenever going away. You could say I was excited to say the least, if slightly nervous. The atmosphere around the ground was aggressive, boisterous and joyful.

As we made the short walk from Fulham Broadway station and the back of the West Stand came into view, my first visit to my second home, at last, became a reality. The queue at the Bovril Gate to gain entry stretched onto the Fulham Road, where we stood for five minutes, stationary. So, Pete said we should head to the main entrance where there were more turnstiles. It wasn't much better, but at least the crowds were moving quicker. A chant went up based on West Ham's anthem:

I'm forever blowing bubbles, pretty bubbles in the air
They fly so high. They reach the sky
And like West Ham, they fade and die
Tottenham always running. Arsenal running too
We're the Chelsea boot boys, and we're running after you!

As we entered the turnstile, paying £1.25 each and trying not to lose my mates, I climbed the stairs into the infamous Shed End. By the time I got to the top, I was hooked and already checking out what other boys were wearing. Skinhead was the look of 1980, and Chelsea's fans were at the forefront of the culture, again. Everywhere you looked, someone had a Green MA1 jacket, rolled-up jeans or DMs, and there was more hair on a snooker ball than the collective heads bouncing about.

Once I reached the top of the stairs, the ground seemed to be twice as big as it looked on *The Big Match*. The sight and sound of The Shed, in full flow, was intoxicating. Following Pete and Greg, myself and Martin walked behind the terrace and the Old Bill platforms towards the West Stand. Greg's old man said we'd get a better view below the Tea Bar and, after navigating through geezers in scarfs, and boot boys and general loutishness, we found a spot halfway down the terrace in the open. I was here, and I'd just seen my future. Excited doesn't even cut it. One thing I did was to take it all in, knowing when to look away when staring too intently at a boot boy or trying to absorb every song, word-for-word, to repeat at school on Monday.

I did know a couple, like *"You're gonna get your fucking head kicked in!"* and *"You're going home in a fucking ambulance!"* picked up through the playground.

Not that Oldham had brought many fans. I soon worked out where their fans were stood, by the massive gaps in the terrace in one of the pens. There were also Chelsea fans in the North Stand, in the pen closest to the West Stand. Well handy for attacking any away fans as they walked past. *"North Stand, North Stand, do your job! North Stand, do your job!"* was an often-heard chant from The Shed.

Chelsea beat Oldham Athletic 3-0 but eventually missed out on promotion on goal difference thanks to West Ham losing at Sunderland, 2 days after winning the F.A. Cup. I was hooked and, from then on in, it became the most important place in my world. Unfortunately, Chelsea's side and poor management saw a real downturn in results. The following three seasons, in the Second Division, became more and more about survival than challenging for the big prizes. I started going to away games as well, and survival at some of these northern outposts was never more keenly felt as it would 'go off' on most occasions.

Chelsea's support away from home was far more partisan and aggressive than the dwindling crowds at Stamford Bridge could offer. Stamford Bridge being half-full back then could make for a poor atmosphere, and most teams brought very few, in terms of numbers to add any spice. As I said earlier, I was no fighter, but I was certainly no runner either. Most of the time, you were more under threat from the local Plod than the other mob. South Yorkshire Police were very happy to let you know who was boss, given the right moment. Step off the pavement in the escort from the station to grounds like Hillsborough, Oakwell or Millmoor, or make threatening gestures to their firm outside their pubs, and crack went the truncheon round your legs. I used to have bruises the size of dinner plates.

And then we'd inevitably lose and, by 6pm, you'd wonder why you'd gone. However, by Wednesday, I was always buzzing for next Saturday's game.

But it wasn't all doom and gloom. In 1982, Chelsea had a cup run and reached the Sixth round of the FA Cup after beating Liverpool, the

European Champions, 2-0 with goals from Peter Rhodes-Brown and Colin Lee. We were then drawn to face our most hated rivals, Tottenham Hotspur. I didn't know why we hated Spurs so much until that day. For me and my mate, Lock, it was QPR. Northolt was a QPR stronghold, and the Boxing Day games were always lively events, especially as we always had fans in three of their stands. Of course, I'd heard stories about the 1967 Cup Final, where we lost 2-1 in the first 'All Cockney' final and fights between 'lads' outside the ground. Also, I knew about the infamous match at White Hart Lane where both teams were fighting relegation, and where aggro broke out before, during and after the game. The respective captains on the day, Steve Perryman and an 18-year-old Ray Wilkins, took the rare step of leading the teams out together to try and bring some sort of calm to proceedings. It mattered not one jot, as flare-wearing loons kicked the fuck out of each other as the teams walk towards the centre circle.

Tottenham won 2-0 and stayed up. We went the other way.

Back to 1982, and the atmosphere that day at Stamford Bridge was one of the best I've ever witnessed. And, in my youthful optimism, I was convinced it was 'our year'. We got into the ground early as this was in the days before we bought advance tickets and it was just as well that we did; the gates shut some 10 minutes later at 1.40 for a 3pm kick Off. Tottenham had also filled the massive away end and that blend of excitement, hate and tension was something extra, something different. The songs from The Shed took on a new meaning:

Hello! Hello! We are the Chelsea boys!
Hello! Hello! We are the Chelsea boys!
And if you are a Tottenham fan, surrender or you'll die
We all follow the Chelsea!

There was also:

The famous Tottenham Hotspur went to Rome to see the Pope
The famous Tottenham Hotspur went to Rome to see the Pope
The famous Tottenham Hotspur went to Rome to see the Pope, and this
is what he said:
"FUCK OFF!"

Or:

Who's that team they call the Chelsea? Who's that team we all adore?
They're the boys in Blue and White and they fight with all their might and
we're out to show the world the way to score!
Bring on Tottenham or the Arsenal. Bring on Scousers by the score.
Barcelona, Real Madrid. Tottenham are a load of ...

And:

You'll never make the station!
You'll never make the station!

As most people know, Tottenham has a Jewish following and became a target for anti-Semitism. Fans at clubs like Chelsea picked up on it. And, of course, we had a sizeable right-wing following which saw the National Front selling copies of their horrible rag, NF News, and the British Movement selling theirs, Bulldog, outside the ground before most games back then. For me and some of my mates, that's something we refused to embrace.

By the time the game kicked off, the whole ground was on a knife edge. Even the East Stand was singing. After a tense 40 minutes, Chelsea was awarded a free kick just outside the area and our star player, Micky Fillery, smacked it home. I've watched football the best part of 45 years and I've still yet to see a crowd go as mad as we did that day. I don't think I stopped jumping up and down till the ref blew the whistle for half time. The buzz was just brilliant; it really felt like it was our year. And, of course, it's the hope that kills you. Their manager, Keith Burkinshaw, must have torn into his players at half-time. Tottenham came out firing for the Second half on that cold March afternoon. Hoddle worked his magic and, before we knew it, Chelsea was 3-1 down. Tottenham were a good side in that era, having won the Cup the year before, and we never really got a look-in after that.

Alan Mayes scored a consolation near the end but, by then, all thoughts had turned to what would happen outside. All the older boys near me were really hyped up for violence and, as we got onto the Fulham Road, the Old Bill had unusually divided the road using barriers, with Chelsea fans ushered onto the pavement across the road from the ground. Chelsea Chairman Ken Bates had produced a programme with a black cover warning fans not to get involved with trouble or there'd be consequences.

Nobody gave a fuck about Cuddly Ken's nonsense and, as we got nearer to the West and North Stand entrances, there was sporadic fighting in the road before the barriers got pushed over and the police had to retreat. This was civil disobedience on a new scale to my young eyes, and very exciting. The two sides were split apart as the police regrouped and I was back on the pavement to the far left, near Fulham Broadway station. Just as I started to walk, out of the corner of my good eye, I saw a glass Lucozade bottle come flying towards me. Luckily, I managed to turn my head as the bottle glanced across it and shattered behind.

"FUCKING TOTTENHAM CUNT!"

Shaken, but not stirred, I made my way into the station, when someone with a terrace trannie, (That's a radio btw, we ain't Dulwich Hamlet) let everyone in earshot know that QPR had beaten Crystal Palace at Loftus Road, which compounded the misery even further.

Tottenham went on to beat QPR in the final that year and a load of us went to the replay. My pal Mark Lyall, being Arsenal, came into his own that day mercifully goading the Spurs fans on the fence in the next block. Until he fell off it. Something he did again some 4 years later a lad's holiday in Tenerife, from the second floor of our hotel. But that's another story.

From that day on, it all made sense why the hatred runs so deep, and there have been too many incidents over the years to ever let me forget that.

I still take absolute delight in Chelsea beating Spurs more than any other club.

English Civil War

I have no real great memories of Ealing Green High School. All that "best days of your life" bollocks. I couldn't be arsed. Most of the education on offer was pointless to me. I started high school with the best of intensions, to pass exams, do well and make the parents proud. But history, geography, physics, chemistry, woodwork and even English bored the absolute shit out of me, which is mad looking back now with this being my fifth book, but my head was elsewhere.

As I was going to watch Chelsea most weekends with Lock, and had got into music big time, being tied to a school that was a fair trot away (a 15-minute walk to Sudbury Hill or South Harrow station, jump onto the Piccadilly Line, change at Ealing Common for Ealing Broadway and then another ten-minute walk to school) didn't mean much after the first year or so.

I loved playing football but never got near the first team and, after a few sub appearances for the second team, didn't even bother turning up for games after a while. By the time I'd reached 14, it was all Micky Fillery, The Jam, Fred Perry's clothing range and falling in love with every bird who looked at me.

Feargal Sharkey was bang on; teenage dreams were hard to beat.

The catalyst for subliminally giving up was a music lesson where the teacher, Mr Crocket, asked the class to bring in a record to play on the school turntable and then discuss its merits. Crocket was posh. Posh to me anyway. He wore a tweed jacket, bow tie and polished brogues.

He played piano in a classical style as often as possible and spoke in a way that seemed to patronise and confuse all at the same time. I didn't like him. In fact, I didn't like any of the teachers apart from Mr. Stevenson, a flare-wearing soul boy who you could easily distract from formal teaching.

So, a chance to show off my new-found tastes.

I was all over that. 1979 was a year for change. I'd gone from the likes of Darts and Boomtown Rats, very quickly, into The Jam, Skids and The Clash. The adrenaline 7" records such as 'Strange Town', 'Masquerade' and 'Tommy Gun' was like letting off tiny bombs in my mind. The morning of the lesson, I bought along The Clash's latest single, 'English Civil War'.

The lesson kicked off with some reggae brought in by a kid from Acton, which passed the teacher by, and he made some sort of snide comment. This was followed with ELO's 'Mr. Blue Sky' and 'Night Fever' by The Bee Gees, which Crocket seemed to approve of, and he played both 7" records in full. He encouraged us to discuss the tracks after and, even though I love them now, I thought they were shit at the time. I just kept quiet. I waited for my song. It would liven the room up, no question.

It was my turn. The Clash were rebels; cool, hard and happening. All the older kids swore by them. I had only just started buying records and punk/new wave was my calling. 'English Civil War', purchased the day before at WH Smith's, is loud, abrasive and confrontational. It was everything I wanted to be, but I was still finding my feet. I was the opposite at that point. The music talked for me though. It filled my senses with an urgency, a sense of purpose and a razor-sharp joy.

The crackle from the needle touching the vinyl, followed by Joe Strummers voice and guitar, fills the air.

However, a classroom of 12 and 13-year-olds were instantly restless:
"What's this crap, Deabill?"
"He can't sing!"
"Bloody punk rubbish!"

Then Mick, Topper and Simmo kick in with the full weight of their nuclear power and Crocket visibly winces.

He takes the record off halfway through and said "That, Deabill, has to be one of the worst things I've ever heard" to a cheering classroom.

He handed me back the vinyl with a pitied grimace as if I had issues.

The only issue I had was being openly mugged off in front of 28 other pupils for doing something that was asked. The stick from other kids I could handle but from an elder who wanted me to share my burgeoning taste with others in a shared experience?

From that day on, I never trusted that wanker, the school system or the middle classes again.

Dawning of a New Era

A while back, my good pal, Simon Kortlang, lent me a book by David Hepworth titled *1971–Never A Dull Moment*, which laid claim to it being the best year in musical history. He'd laid down a marker of huge significance in which it would take a more skilled writer than myself to even put a dent in his conviction. But, even after having my head turned, I'd still say the best year for music and its cultural impact in my own lifetime is 1979.

In recent years, it's been scientifically proven that the music that hits you between the ages of 13 and 14 is what you'll carry, forever. I say science. It's probably written by one of BBC 6 Music's northern DJs, of which there are far too many. However, that is unquestionably true in my case. Being 13 in 1979, I can't think of a more brilliant year for discovering music and the fashion that went with my own calling. It was a year of change, musically, politically and personally. The year Thatcher started her assault on the British working class.

Although I'd seen and heard music through TV stuff like *Supersonic*, *Saturday Scene* and *Top of the Pops*, it didn't really enter my head to start buying or asking for songs I liked until 1977. So, with some record tokens I'd received for my birthday, I bought *Disco Fever*, a K-Tel compilation, which seemed like a 'cool' thing to have, even if the sleeve, with its badly dressed revellers, screamed anything but. Twenty big hits in a value-for-money, all-in-one package. After a few plays, it dawned on me I only really liked The Boomtown Rats 'Lookin' After No. 1', mainly for its energy and punk attitude.

Punk appealed because the main protagonists, The Sex Pistols, swore and upset the establishment. Naughty.

Earlier that summer, I'd become taken with the Eddie and The Hot Rods classic, 'Do Anything You Wanna Do', which seemed to crash out of the radio speakers in glorious surround sound with its anthemic vocal escapism and spiky guitars.

Punk might have raged across pockets of the UK but, apart from 'Pretty Vacant', I'd yet to feel the full force, especially as all the classics were given a swerve on daytime radio. Again, like the Hot Rods, the urgency made me jump up and down and stick two fingers out of the window to that miserable wanker, Mr Evans across the road.

This is when my mum and dad had gone shopping because it was the only time that used my dad's Technics system. He was a bit touchy about an 11-year-old messing up his settings!

That was my introduction to rebellion. Trampy, shouty, pyjama-wearing freaks from Dublin and strange-looking blokes from Essex. By 1978, I went backwards and bought 'You're the One That I Want' by John and Olivia (I just fancied her rotten thanks to Grease, where she goes all filthy at the end), and 50s throwbacks, Darts, and *The Amazing Darts* LP on cassette.

I still can't work that one out. 'Daddy Cool' was no 'Ever Fallen in Love'. With no older brother to steer me clear of poor musical choices, my cousin, Claire, saved me, lending me singles such as The Stranglers,'5 Minutes', and The Jam's 'Down in the Tube Station at Midnight'. This showed me the path out of the murky waters.

The Clash were the doyens of older kids at school with taste. Someone had graffitied their name all over the bogs and they were almost spoken about in reverential terms, hence why I was drawn to them. And my passion for The Jam has been well documented in my first book, *'Thick as Thieves – Personal Situations with The Jam'*.

Clothes-wise, I was becoming as aware of the fast-changing times for fashion as I was of music. No longer were clothes bought for me, nor was I drawn to wearing cap-sleeve tees just because The Fonz did. I was desperate for a Harrington Jacket to go with my Levi's, bought from Dickie Dirts, and my Adidas Samba trainers bought from Northolt Sports. After trying to explain to Mum and Dad what type of jackets they were, the old man took us down to Wembley Market and bought the iconic piece of clothing. It was only some years later that I learnt why it was called a Harrington, after the Baracuta G9 jacket in the US soap opera, *Peyton Place*, as worn by character Rodney Harrington. The outerwear was first seen over on these shores in the late 60s, worn by skinheads and lingering modernists.

Pocket money was now increasingly being spent on 7" records bought from Sellanby and Woolworths on Northolt Road, South Harrow. As my confidence in being out and about grew, trying to be a 'face', so did my light fingers. Woolies, the training ground for any young tea leaf, became an unknowing benefactor to my growing record collection. There was a thrill, seeing new stock arrive, and the fantastically bright and striking record bags became a beacon for my magpie eyes.

New Wave heroes, such as The Members, Buzzcocks, The Ruts and Skids, were regularly lighting up *Top of the Pops* with their quirky, powerful performances. 'Masquerade' from the Dunfermline four-piece Skids was my first taste of the new angular pop sound. Stuart Adamson's guitar lines proper bent my head. Also, frontman Richard Jobson looked like he could explode at any minute. I was still some way off trying to describe how Masquerade sounded. I just fucking loved it! Same as The Ruts 'Babylon's Burning'. What a tune! Lead singer Malcolm Owen came from neighbouring town Southall and their first gig was in The Target pub, where the McDonalds now stands. "With ignorance and hate!" Yes Malc!

After my first year of high school, it was the family's annual trip down to New Milton in Dorset, to stay at my gran's chalet. It was during that stay, just after I turned 13, when I first heard 'Gangsters' by The Special AKA. For someone who had never heard Ska music before, the sound was a true revelation to me. In fact, I was hearing a new sound every week, be it Tubeway Army, Motorhead or The Flying Lizards. The chart was so diverse at that time.

TOTP, as ever the gateway to the pop world, featured Thin Lizzy next to The Dooleys, next to Chic, next to Matchbox, next to Errol Dunkley, etc. The music finds you though, right? It's up there in the sky, searching for the spirit of the individual before filling their mind where they should be heading.

Hearing 'Gangsters' for the second time backed up my initial thoughts that it was mind-blowing.

On returning to Northolt, Wardy, a kid a year below me in Greenwood, shouted out of his bedroom window, asking if I'd heard it while furiously chomping through a lemon Jubbly. He then showed me his copy, with the iconic 2 Tone paper sleeve, and I lied, "*Yeah I've got it. Good innit!*" I thought, "*Fucking hell! Wardy's a knob. I've got to buy a copy now!*"

The next day, I cycled up to Sellanby, through Roxeth Park (which we called South Harrow Park), down Kingsley Road, and chained the trusty Grifter to a lamppost. The magic of a record shop for me back then brought a sense of wonder, not knowing what you might hear in there, who you might see and, without sounding like an old perv, the lovely smell of vinyl.

Sellanby was run by two brothers who traded in second-hand vinyl but sold new stuff too. Unfortunately, they came with, what I thought was a hippie sensibility, which was basically anything between 1967 and 1976 in my underdeveloped mind. For some strange reason though that day, I swerved on one of the greatest debut singles of all time - and bought 'Bang Bang' by BA Robertson. What was I thinking?

Well, it was a catchy ditty about unsolicited sexual liaisons, but fucking hell! He looked like a wrong 'un as well. One of those geezers who loved the biz, acting like a right cock on the telly. About as cool as Terry Wogan's collars.

It didn't dawn on me to take it back and swap it. I was too shy. It wasn't in the racks at Woolies, so I couldn't nick it, and M.J. Parkes in the Parade, at the other end of Northolt Road, only had a small selection of records for sale among the greeting cards, stationery and other shit it sold. Not one of life's happier people. He was a right grumpy old wanker and his eyes followed you with every second spent on his premises.
I had to wait for next week's pocket money to own a copy.

Once purchased, it didn't leave the turntable for ages. Also, after seeing them in *Smash Hits* and then on *Top of the Pops*, the look engulfed me - the suits, the Fred Perry shirts, the white socks and the loafers. And it hadn't gone unnoticed that the clobber could sit nicely underneath the school blazer.

Hartex, the cut-price clothing shop, again on the Northolt Road, sold all the gear needed - black sta-prest trousers, white button-down Ben Sherman shirts (size 15-and-a-half), white and red towelling socks and the piece de resistance, Frank Wright tassel loafers. Always work from the shoes up. I looked and felt the bollocks, going into school on the first day back. Being a 3rd year had two advantages. I wasn't a new boy anymore and you could see other kids' identities and personalities coming through.

We were the so-called Grange Hill generation, but a lot smarter than those scruffs Tucker, Benny and Alan Humphries. David Russell looked like Paul Weller's younger brother, especially with the Gibson black-and-white shoes that he constantly slipped about in. Clever Trevor had a pair of trousers that seemed to change colour!
Tonics became the stride to be seen in.

Soul Boy Steve wore grey flannels and burgundy patent slip-ons with big, flicky hair. Black kids were rocking the short dread look, playing the likes of Bob Marley and Front-Line reggae compilation cassettes in the classroom wherever possible.

The comprehensive playground slowly became awash with artifacts and labels of the era. Most tried to keep within the strict uniform code because you could get dug out by the ex-grammar school teachers, who loved a bit of caning and slippering, the sick fucks.

The next band to come into my life was Madness.

A youthful Suggs grinning like a mutant cat on amphetamine and doing that shuffle was just fantastic. And he wasn't much older than me! How could you not move to 'The Prince'?

The rise of 2 Tone was meteoric in that short space of time. Everyone was on it. Girls and boys. Black and white. Unite and fight. After reading an *NME* article about Ska and understanding it was the precursor to reggae, it was soon another stepping stone into a lifelong love.

The re-releases of 'Skinhead Moonstomp' and 'Liquidator' meant my generation could understand why 1969 was important, musically and culturally, and black and white did mix, at least before the bonehead mob divided everybody and spread their hate. The brilliant film, '*Quadrophenia*', fully kicked in a Mod Revival that The Jam had started some time back. There weren't too many Mods over my way, and the ones who went down that road were usually a bit tapped.

Further singles from 2 Tone included The Selecter's 'On My Radio' and The Specials' 'A Message to You, Rudy', a Dandy Livingstone cover. On the flip was 'Nite Klub', a song so infectious, it should come with a health warning. By the time The Specials self-titled album hit the stands, 2 Tone was the most important movement to hit the UK's streets since punk. Every kid I know loved it.

On a sidenote, I always admired the strange fey kid who was a massive Gary Numan fan and a card-carrying Numanoid, with his parted hair, diagonal buttoned shirt and strange walk. And, naturally, he was a punch bag for the bullies.

There was a resident association under-16 disco at St Barnabas Church Hall on the Fairway, where the DJ played 'Gangsters' and all the kids danced so hard, the needle jumped every five seconds. By the end of the year, I'd played the album so often, Mum and Dad knew every word, whether they liked it or not. And by Christmas, I'd just started my first job as a paper boy at The Top Shop and had even more records coming into the house.

'Message In A Bottle' on green vinyl by The Police. The Beat's 'Tears of a Clown'. Squeeze's 'Up the Junction', on pink vinyl. 'Don't Stop 'Til You Get Enough' by Michael Jackson. 'Accidents Will Happen' by Elvis Costello and The Attractions. Madness's 'One Step Beyond' on 12". 'Money In My Pocket' by Dennis Brown. 'Silly Games' by Janet Kay. Chic's 'Good Times'. 'London Calling' by The Clash. '17' by The Regents and loads of other outstanding audio treats. Not 'Another Brick in the Wall' though. Pink Floyd was still the hippies amongst us and Rotten told us that we should 'never trust a hippy'.

The tribalism of youth feels like it's gone forever now (Mods, Punks, Teds, Rockabilly's, Rude Boys and Girls, Skins, Soul Boys and Girls, Dreads, Numanoids, Smellies, Headbangers, etc.). Even though it didn't always feel like it, for me and my generation, I feel we had the best of it.

1979.
Best. Year. Ever.

Wardy the Punk

David Ward, of 1 Clauson Avenue was the neighbourhood menace.

He had a fruit machine in his box room, which stunk of fags and wank tissues, and he had a penchant for playing lower league punk, such as Anti-Nowhere League and their sweary 'So What?', at ear-splitting volume with the speakers facing out of his front window.

He also had green spiky hair, would gob at passers-by and hide underneath the open window, cackling, calling people cunts and making strange bird noises. He was a good laugh for a bit but the sort of kid who'd cause aggro / chaos just by walking down the road. He was also a fist and old bill magnet as well. A one-off.

One Saturday in early 1980, I travelled by train to see my Nan and Grandad in Marlow, with Wardy the Punk. Wardy was a law onto himself, green spiky hair, studded leather jacket, DMs, and an annoying twat. I'm in a Harrington, Toniks and Monkey Boots, all from Wembley Market.

God knows what my grandparents thought of him. I knew exactly what my mum and dad thought of him.

Anyway, once we'd trotted round the town, the only place of interest was the record shop. Whilst in there I bought the latest 12" by Madness, 'My Girl'. Wardy just gobbed on the floor as it didn't have any U.K. Subs or Angelic Upstarts.

When we got back to my grans flat, she made us a cup of tea and asked me what was in the bag.

I muttered under my breath "You don't want to know."
"Oh yes I do, Stuart! Shall we play it?"

I'm 13, awkward, and burning up. Play my gran the latest release by Madness? The Nutty Boys? Marjorie was very straight and not one for silliness.

Wardy just encouraged it, catching on to my embarrassment. (I'm here all week). "Yes, play it! Play it Stu's gran!"

So, reluctantly I put the record on the dark age 'music centre' and let the needle do its thing.

For three minutes, it felt like an episode of *Juke Box Jury* as Granny Slade contemplated her considered opinion. As the last note rang out, she said in a voice not too dissimilar to Mrs Bouquet from *Keeping Up Appearances*. "It's not very good, is it?"

I cringed some more.

Wardy just put two fingers up to me behind her back, cackling his head off.

I put the record back in the sleeve, finished my tea, and made our excuses that we had to get back as Wardy's Mum was expecting him home for football practice. (He was fucking useless at sport).

On the train back Mr Ward was peaking in the annoying stakes, by doing his bird noises at the top of his voice to various passengers. I somehow managed to escape from him at Ealing Broadway, where we changed trains. In the short time we waited for a District Line he got collared by the station plod for starting a fire on the platform with discarded newspapers 'to keep warm' - I was well down the platform when he got tugged, thank fuck.

Parklife

My first job was with a company called Oakley Farm in Perivale, two stops down the Central Line from Northolt. Having left school without any qualifications that summer, I didn't have many options. I would have been happy on the dole for a bit as there were alternatives available that weren't strictly kosher. My old man wasn't having it, so it was Job Centre time for me, and the dreaded government funded YOP Scheme at £25 a week.

The Youth Opportunity Scheme, brought in by Labour PM James Callaghan in 1978, was a stopgap to null the effect of so many school leavers going straight on the dole and to help 16 to 18-year-olds into cheap labour employment. When Thatcher got in a year later, she made it a permanent fixture called the Youth Training Scheme (YTS).

Oakley Farm packed and delivered frozen food, fruit and veg orders to company canteens across the South East. To be honest, it wasn't a bad place to start the long and tedious graft career. Everyone hated each other so you knew where you stood from the off. My official title was Warehouse Operative, so it was basically putting incoming deliveries away into chillers and walk-in freezers. And, of course, the two older geezers who worked in the warehouse took great delight in locking me in the freezer whenever possible as some sort of initiation. I got my own back wherever possible by hiding their coats in skips or eating their sandwiches.

In the run-up to 5th November, me and my pals had decided to have our own bonfire and my part of the bargain was to get the necessary wood from work. I asked my boss if it was OK to use the broken pallets for a resident's association firework party and, because he admired my community spirit, he was more than happy to help me.

He told one of the delivery drivers, Mick, to give me a lift back to Northolt with the broken pallets on Friday afternoon. We loaded the 7.5-ton lorry, with the company logo plastered all over it, and took the short journey from Perivale to 'The Big Park' so called because there were two parks in Russell Road, with the smaller one imaginatively titled The Little Park. It was the usual chat about what we were up to over the weekend, and Mick was excited about how pissed he was going to get, and shag Jen the barmaid in The Millet Arms who apparently 'swallowed'.

Looking like Mike Randall from *Randall & Hopkirk (Deceased)*, I doubted Jen would let the likes of smelly old Mick anywhere near her, never mind have his bollocks on her chin.

As we pulled up outside the park, I opened the gates and told him to back up to the playground at the top of the short path. It was around 4pm and still daylight, and Mick kept asking me if this was a kosher display.

"Yeah, yeah – all good mate".

As we unloaded the broken pallets, he looked at me and said, "If this ain't right, I'll fucking do ya!" with a wry laugh and for the first time, he saw my face drop and screamed "You facking cunt, Stu. I'm off!"

He drove out of the park a lot quicker than I'd seen him move in the short time I'd been working there.

I went home to catch the first episode of a brand-new music show, *The Tube*, which had kickstarted the new Channel 4 for me that evening, whilst trying not to drop my dinner down me as The Jam played live. Buoyed up by the best band in the fucking land, heading towards the last stretch of their career, I told Mum I was off to a display and that I'd see her later.

We all met up over The Big Park about 7pm. It had rained over the previous hour and therefore made the pallets difficult to light. The Big Park was our theatre of dreams; the legendary 15-a-side games between the nicked full-size goalposts and enclosed by the nicked line paint laid down by the nicked paint machine. In the summer, we marked out the cricket pitch with the nicked lawnmower and kept score with the nicked scoreboard. (Big thanks to Harrow Cricket Club and Harrow Council for the lend of their gear.)

We'd already had a whip round and bought all the fireworks that a tenner could cover, and we were all looking forward to being little teenage bastards. Unfortunately, we went through about four packs of Swan Vesta trying to light the wet wood and frustration set in.

However, Paddy had the bright idea of heading to Petts Hill petrol station to fill up the jerry can his old man had left lying in his back garden.

Within 30 minutes, and with the four-star strategically poured over the broken pallets, the caveman thrill of fire took hold.

Manic giggling set in as the Kestrel lager and Strongbow cider helped the buzz along. In fact, the wood went up so well, it started melting the nearby metal climbing frame as the flames reached over 15 foot high. We were admiring our work when we heard sirens. Next thing, someone screamed out from their back garden "You little shits! The fire brigade and the police are on their way!"

We all looked at each other and the shout went up:
"LEG IT!".

Twelve of us sprinted towards the massive oak trees at the top of the park, leapt over the fence, sprinted down the back alley into Clauson Avenue and we all faded into the night in different directions, back to our homes and away from a very likely nick for arson and criminal damage.

The next morning, I went to The Big Park with my hood up to see what damage we might have caused. We'd done a good job of destroying a playground. Sorry kids. A melted metal tank frame, scorched tarmac, burnt remnants of Standard rockets and charred wood with the branded markings of 'Property of Oakley Farm' still visible.

On Monday, Mick asked how the weekend went. I wasn't going to tell him that the local plod and fire brigade turned up mob handed. He'd have gone fucking mental and probably grassed.

"Not bad, mate. We didn't have it in the end," I lied. "What about you, Mick?"

"Yeah. Shagged Jen, didn't I?"

Time for Heroes

Summer Summer 1982. I'd just left school. Looking for something to do, a few of us went up to Ruislip Lido, where some mates were going for a row with some rocker/psychobilly types, probably from Harrow. The pub, The Roxborough on College Road, was always full of them. All King Kurt patches and coloured spiky hair, or GI flat tops and sleeveless denim jackets. Ooh Wallah Wallah indeed! Not sure why we'd decided to get involved but we was probably hoping they would be a few girls about.

Although I'd seen the odd person in expensive sportswear attire, it never hit me until I got off the bus, and among the Adidas Kagoules and Levi's which most of us were sporting, that there was this fella I vaguely knew from school, who stood out like a streetlamp on a dark cold night. Wearing a navy cashmere Pringle jumper with red and white diamonds, faded Lois jeans and Adidas Wimbledon trainers, he looked amazing. Of course, all the detail came after closer inspection, but I was born with an eye for detail. I couldn't take my eyes off the sweater.

I never imagined something that Bernard Gallagher, Nick Faldo or even Ronnie Corbett would wear could ever rock my world. The kid was even first in for the tear up, so he became a cult hero, in my eyes, in an instant.

That was my introduction into the world of *Casual*. The term was still a way off but, for us, it was a sort of soul boy look. Loads of the older kids had gone in for the wedge haircut matched with lairy short-sleeved shirts, Fiorucci jeans or Farah slacks, and patent leather shoes. It was a look regularly seen cruising about Northolt in a Ford Capri or an Escort XR3i, with the latest American imports bouncing out of the speakers via the latest mix cassettes by the likes of Froggy, a big DJ name around the manor. The 2 Tone rude boy look had long gone, and Adidas had become the main staple. Adidas Sambas, Levi's, Adidas Cali tees and MA1 jackets were more my thing.

I'd recently bought a pair of Adidas Hawaii trainers, which looked good with the grey Farah slacks (well, in my head anyway) but I was desperate to have a Pringle jumper. After having a look in a couple of golf shops and being totally dismayed by the prices, obtaining one was going to take a lot longer than anticipated. While on holiday in Bournemouth with the family, we went into this big department store and there were plain coloured Pringles in the August sale!

With some birthday dough and the old man finally opening his wallet, I managed to purchase a plain light blue v-neck. The buzz of putting that jumper on, with the Farah slacks and Hawaii trainers, made me feel I was unique, special, and I walked round the chalet park that night feeling untouchable.

By the time the football season started, I realised quickly that I was just one of many who had followed the road to Damascus (Stuarts, Moda and other dedicated emporiums) over the summer, and all my mates were on board with the expensive sportswear look.

As Chelsea were struggling in the Second Division at the time, the away days to Rotherham and Leeds became fashion parades, not only to show the home fans the way forward dress-wise, but also to show off the latest garments. It eventually became far more important than the games because we were shocking on the pitch.

In September, I started work on £25 a week and, after bunging my mum some money, was left with 15 notes. As most items were out of my league, you had to spend wisely. It helped that the local golf shops got broken into on a regular basis and, if you were quick, you'd hear that one of the lads had some Lyle & Scott bits for sale. The opportunities were few and far between. It was rare a Fila BJ Matchday Velour tracksuit top would come your way.

I started buying and selling records, amongst other things, so that helped to keep the wardrobe fresh. The clobber became a massive part of my young life. I'd started to become a regular in Stuarts, and my namesake would always drop a fiver off the retail price for me whilst giving me a sneak preview into what was coming in next week.

Thanks to John McEnroe's Sergio Tacchini gear, I decided that I'd start buying some of their pieces. It wasn't as heavily worn as Fila round my way.

I bought a white with black stripe Waffle Orion tracksuit, which instantly became the most impressive item in my wardrobe. I felt that good wearing it to Marcia Baillie's 18th birthday party at Harrow Cricket Club, I expected to be batting the women off into extra cover with a shitty stick, especially as my hair was at the right length for me to flick it out of my eye for added drama. That was until Phil Nolan pulled the bottoms down when I was holding two pints in front of the whole function room. Luckily, my pants stayed in place and my old chap wasn't given a major airing. (Thank fuck we didn't have camera phones back then.) I never wore those bottoms out again!

Chelsea saved themselves from relegation at Bolton towards the end of the 1982/83 season, where I had managed to spill coffee on my new beige diamond Lyle & Scott jumper on the train. It made me feel like a tramp for the rest of the day. Still, the result more than made up for it, as Clive 'Flasher' Walker got the winner and sent the travelling support garrity.

So, we all looked forward to the new season, as chairman Ken Bates and our brilliant manager, Johnny Neal pulled in some decent players such as Pat Nevin, Nigel Spackman, Kerry Dixon and Eddie Niedzwiecki, during the close season. On the opening day, at Stamford Bridge, we smashed Derby 5-0.

When I looked around the West Stand benches that afternoon, it seemed like every kid was wearing a label of some sort. A sea of pastel.

I'd bought some Lois cords and split the hem to give them extra width over my new trainers; the classic Diadora Borg Elites. The kangaroo leather made them feel like you were on the bounce. Very handy if you had to avoid a police baton or run a mob up the road.

Also, the ubiquitous Kicker (or Noddy) boot became a staple on the trotter front. Liverpudlian Kevin Sampson wrote an article in *The Face* magazine during that long hot summer of 1983, which gave the likes of us a name - 'Casual' and it stuck. And Chelsea were very 'Casual'. We had that swagger that the clothes gave you, and the confidence to carry it off as we strode purposely around alien streets. Do you want fruit in that bowl, son?

And we also had a team that had swagger in abundance on the pitch for the first time since the early 70s. The fans turned out in droves in cities and towns such as Sheffield, Manchester, Blackburn and Derby to get behind the team, as well as to take as many liberties as possible.

We were doing the business on the pitch, on the terraces and on the clobber front. I loved every second of that season, getting back into the local to give it large after an arduous train journey home from some hick town and people asking you how much the Fila mohair jumper you were styling cost (though when Lock bought an identical one, I nearly cried. He didn't get it the same way as I did. It was an unwritten rule to never copy your pal's threads. Though he never did it again).

To be part of a burgeoning cult that was fresh and new, and to wear clobber that wasn't readily available in other parts of the country, all added to our London-centric confidence and arrogance.

Chelsea were promoted as Second Division champions and the first game of the 1984/85 season was Arsenal away! I'd never been to Highbury before, and Chelsea were given the whole of the Clock End. To me, it was the defining moment of being a teenage Chelsea Casual - 15,000 crammed into that end with more dotted about the other three stands, and most of those golden faces were under 25, all dressed to impress.

And the buzz when Kerry Dixon scored was off the scale. Check YouTube for how mental we all go! A close second to the atmosphere at Stamford Bridge at half time against Spurs.

Later that season, the real high-end gear, such as Giorgio Armani jumpers and Burberry golf jackets, paved the way forward and away from the tracksuits. But, when Kerry Dixon smashed that iconic goal into the top corner on that steamy summer day, the whole end of youths with wedged haircuts, Lacoste and Gee2 polo shirts, Lois cords and Fiorucci jeans went absolutely barmy. It still gives me goosebumps to this day.

As the season went on, the clothes became more garish and colourful. I remember an ill-thought-out outfit of an overhead leather three-colour patchwork jacket, pink Pringle polo and canary yellow cords worn with grey Trimm Trabs.

No wonder the old man thought I was on the turn.

As the 80s progressed and I got more into bands like New Order, The Smiths and Echo and The Bunnymen, that sort of style was put on hold and I was more drawn to Camden Market clobber; half-zip sweats, MA1 jacket, DM shoes and Hardcore jeans. That rare groove warehouse party look took hold around 1987. Thank fuck I saw the light around the turn of the decade as a certain Massimo Osti and the beauty of Stone

Island, Bonneville and CP Company clobber came into my life, thanks to meeting an Arsenal face who could supply the gear at half price.

"Just when you thought you was out, they pull you back in".

Wonder what happened to that kid in the cashmere Pringle though?

Just Who Is the 5 o'Clock Hero?

Work, by and large, is shit. You might do a job that is passable and doesn't give you the fear on a Sunday night but, unless you're of simple stock, earning large for doing very little, Captain in your own industry or just hate your home life so much that grafting is a welcome relief, the daily grind is tedious, annoying and a downright inconvenience.

There can be the odd exception to this but, for me, it's only when I look back at a past occupation. I was a postman between 1984 and 1988, and the craic was something I'll always hold dear.

Health & Safety, was a long way from where it is today. Nobody taught you the correct procedure to lift a mailbag or ride a bike, and you wouldn't be threatened with the sack if you told a customer to fuck off. In fact, one manager actively encouraged it! The bikes are now non-existent, and you never see a postman carrying two full sacks these days either (insert your own joke here).

The job itself, to outsiders, is what you see. You deliver letters, you don't get offers of sex (well, Jonesy did, but more of that later) and you rarely get a cup of tea as you go from door-to-door in all weathers.

But inside the sorting office with 40 posties, working side-by-side separating the mail and then dividing your walk (postal round) before hitting the streets was the best laugh I've had doing a bit of collar – even if you had to be in work for a brutal 5am start.

Introducing some of Greenford Post Office's finest:
Sucker – A low-rent Jack Nicholson lookalike who would sidle up to both men and women whilst sorting their walk, grab hold of his bollocks and grumble in a low tone, "Give us a suck!" then cackle like Sid James on crystal meth.

Jonesy – A young, lazy and workshy Morrissey obsessive who was always late and the only part-timer in our depot. Jonesy just wouldn't do a second delivery. Nothing too unremarkable there except his flat top and lizard-type tongue, for some reason, made him attractive to older men. He was propositioned a few times in the period I worked with him.

One gentleman tried to get him into his car one morning whilst Jonesy was walking to work down Oldfield Lane. Jonesy collars me - Don't say nothing, but this geezer just tried to pull me into his car while he was touching himself. Reckons he'd seen me for a few weeks, and that I looked 'the type'.

By 6am, the whole depot knew and absolutely slaughtered him. He refused to talk to me for a couple of weeks. One colleague even followed Dave into work, driving slowly behind just to put the shits up him.

Bennett – A comedian who would crack you up as soon as he opened his gob. One of his favourite lines was "I leave out more than you get in son" if one of the other lads was talking about last night's conquest from Oscar's. Gift of the gab and great company. Unless you'd been given more overtime than him, then he'd bleat like a herd of sheep on a crumbling cliff, letting every fucker know that he'd been shafted and mugged off.

Reg – Similar to Bennett, but bigger and unshakable. He used to tell us he was a Third Division footballer but couldn't say who for as we'd bother him for his autograph. He'd sit in the Post Office Club and shout out "Oi! Superthug!", which was my nickname because I was always talking about the off at Chelsea the previous weekend.

"Come here. I've got something to tell you".

"Fuck off, Reg! You're going to grab my head and fart".

"No. It's important. It's about the weekly pools" (Precursor to the National Lottery - ask your weird uncle, kids)

I'd walk over there and as soon as you were within five metres, he'd get your head and force it towards his massive, grey-slacked covered 'aris and let off a primeval emission that could instantly turn bread into toast Cheers Reg!

Bob Pervert – Bob would fix the bikes instead of doing a second delivery, which enabled him to double up as keeper of the office's porn collection. For some reason, people used to put *Razzle* and *Fiesta* into the post boxes and, anytime a postie came back with a couple shoved in his sack, Bob had the ability to sniff them out (probably because most of them were stuck together at some point) and claim them for the bike shed. You could loan them, but Bob would write down what you had taken and warn you not to nick them.

Whatever happened to the Polaroid picture that Harry brought back is a mystery though. Why someone would take a picture of a freshly wanked penis with spunk all over the windowsill is beyond me, but we did have some wrong un's at our place.

Bob once opened a package for his female neighbour which had the shape of a big vibrator. The look of disappointment when it turned out to be a shower head was like watching a child having its Happy Meal whipped away.

Denyer – The postal cadet who used to freak out if he had a busy day. Because he started an hour later, the mail would mount up on his desk and we'd start chipping away at him as he tried to sort it into roads for the walk. He'd normally only had 4 hours of sleep after being on the herb for most of the previous day and was very tetchy. Everyone would chip in with comments.

"Busy day there, son?"
"Jesus! You won't be finished until gone 11 with that lot, mate".
"Fuck me! You want to see the number of recorded deliveries you've got!"
"Fucking hell, mate! You should have gone sick".

Suddenly you'd hear "YOU CAAANNTTSS!" as more mail dropped onto his desk. Denyer would then throw all his mail up in the air and shout, "Fuck this!" then storm outside for a fag. All of us would be banging on the sorting frames, cheering as he'd cracked under pressure yet again.

Jenny – Looked like Olive from On The Buses with a complexion like a cheese grater and wouldn't stop moaning in her monotone voice. Unfortunately for Jen, she had the walk next to Sucker, who would regularly torment her - "Oi Jenny! Get down on that!" as he gripped his piece with his tongue out, Kiss-style. Thankfully for Sucker, she didn't go to the Sex Discrimination Board. We think it's the only male attention she ever got, bless her.

Bing – A smart old fella who was a trainspotter in his spare time and used to get visibly excited if he had mail. Even if it was a bill. He absolutely loved working on the post. He had every First Day Cover (Special envelope printed on day of release – Yes very weird Uncle job) from 1953 or something, took pride in his job and his appearance, and was ultimately one of the most boring bastards you'll ever meet.

Fab Five Freddy – The opposite of Bing, a lovely fella but avoided the bath as much as possible. I'd like to say it was because he'd spent most of the afternoon in the bookies with his 50p each-way bets, but it was probably more to do with trying to save on water, the tight fuck.

Smelly Alan – He made Fred smell radiant. Strange guy in his 50's who was softly spoken and hated the youth element. Lived at home with mother, who obviously didn't know what a washing machine was. Tide marks on the neck and a yellow hue on his light blue shirt collars.

Fat Mick (The Union Rep) – Obese bloke who was useless as a postman, and as our depot representative. Lock, who joined me at Greenford, ran for the position in the annual vote and surprisingly won. It upset Mick so much, he went sick for three months. Lock was an incendiary fucker though and probably tried to lead us out on strike over something trivial like the quality of cheese in the work canteen. After getting bored with meetings and arguing, relinquished his position and Mick got voted back in the next year.

Charlie – A diminutive, wire-haired bespectacled Glaswegian with a temper, whose love of Speedway would make him ride his bike like he was on the cinder track at Rye House. Unfortunately, the streets of Greenford had a few potholes, and one day, he came back to the depot clutching his head and broken bins to the sound of derision, laughter and general banter. Charlie, wasn't happy and offered the whole depot outside, which caused even more hilarity, especially when Bennett shouted, "What you gonna do, son? Punch our knees in?"

D'Souza (The Assistant Manager) – A horrible short-arsed fucker who would stitch you up at the drop of a hat. No backbone and no bollocks. If you ever asked him something he didn't want to hear, he'd start shaking with fear and put you on a disciplinary. On the day I left, in June 1988, I brought in a bottle of whiskey, as was the ritual. After two large glasses, I asked him to step outside. It wasn't big or clever, but I felt it had to be done. He screamed like a girl, and I was ushered off the premises by a couple of older and wiser heads. As I walked through the heavy black doors for the last time, he told me from a distance that I'd never work for the Royal Mail again.

He was right!

Live and Dangerous

Bootlegs. When you've exhausted all the albums and singles of your favourite band, the next place to further your passion is unofficial recordings. The real connoisseur collected vinyl boots, but for paupers like me, it was live and session recordings on cassette.

After seeing an ad in the back of the *NME* for exclusive Jam live recordings, I sent off an SAE (stamped addressed envelope, remember them?) and received a 'catalogue' back of 70/80 different Jam gigs from 1977 to 1982.

In the early days, the Woking Wonders' set would fill a C46 – a 46-minute tape cassette, 23 minutes either side. By early 1978, it was a C60, and by 1980 the gigs would be long enough for a C90. They were always hit and miss on quality, as many were recorded by people in the crowd holding up a microphone attached to a tape recorder underneath their coat. Most bands hated them, as the quality didn't do them any favours in their eyes, but for people like me – pure obsessives – it mattered not one iota. Even better when they'd capture Paul berating the crowd and getting lairy.

After buying most of the cassettes available, I decided to purchase a tape-to-tape deck, so I could knock up copies and bang them out, through ads in the NME. Before long I'd started buying up other bands I loved, such as The Smiths and New Order, from sellers in and around Camden Market.

One fella, Big Al, was bang at it, and would print a special illuminous inlay sleeve so his tapes would stand out on his stall on the high street, opposite the market. There were also the two passive aggressive geezers on the corner of Delaney Street, and a junkie dude in the Electric Ballroom we'd buy off. But Al and Chris were the daddies. And New Order was their favourite band. They always had the highest quality, latest recordings.

Chris was also a tout and we used to see him at both gigs and football all over London (and still do), and we became matey. He told me that Al knew exactly where to sit or stand at most venues to get the best sound. Usually in front of the mixing desk.

With Lock, I'd go up once a month to pick up the new gig tapes and then add them to our catalogues. There was a shop in South Harrow that used to supply us TDK tapes in bulk, and at one point in the mid-80s I was making 150 quid a week, which was more than my post office wages.

The next logical step was to buy a Sony Walkman Professional and start recording the gigs ourselves. We'd been all over the UK following The Smiths and so we thought let's see if we can get our trips paid for.

The first gig Lock and I bootlegged was Lloyd Cole and the Commotions at Hammersmith Odeon, and we had a verbal ruck over who should record it. I won that and soon realised after half an hour of positioning a mic towards the stage – without talking and, more importantly, without drinking – that it wasn't that exciting.

After a while we both went our separate ways on the selling front and, by 1987, I lost interest in the whole thing. It was easier to buy and sell tickets to make dough than fuck about with cassettes. Mega gigs like Bruce Springsteen and Michael Jackson at Wembley Stadium fetched good dough, and as it was a 15-minute bus ride away, I was usually on the first number 92 to queue up with all the other spivs with a mate to secure a four- or six-per-person allocation. If you worked it right, and put a different jacket on, you would buy the briefs and either push into the queue to go round again, or if you saw someone you knew or who was easy-going you'd ask them how many they were getting and give them the dough to sort out another pair.

This could cause issues, as we all know that few people like touts. But it's one of the oldest art forms of the streets, and I always looked at it as a service. And compared to nowadays where you don't even have to leave the house, it was always graft in my eyes, with the constant potential to lose money.

It also didn't help matters when we made up a load of U2 C90s to sell outside their biggest ever UK show at that point, Milton Keynes Bowl in June 1985. However, we were struggling to get any takers in the drizzle and then upset a coachload of Island Records staff, who, when getting off the coach, were faced with me, trying to sell them their own band back to them, in the most basic of liberty-taking form.

After a while, we threw the tapes back in the motor, driven by another mate, Dean, and went into watch The Ramones (who were amazing), The Faith Brothers, Billy Bragg and a very excitable Bono and crew. Bono had this habit of climbing the speaker stacks during the track 'The Electric Co.', which, according to Ian 'Mac' McCulloch from the Bunnymen, was like watching "a soddin mountain goat". It was hard to disagree, as we watched the mulletted Dubliner singing away in his stack-heeled boots from a vantage point so high he could've seen his Irish birthplace.

In the mid-90s I picked up the bootleg bug again and hooked up with a mate to sell VHS copies of Weller, Oasis and Primal Scream live gigs and TV compilation videos. That went well until 1997, when we got stung by the British Phonographic Industry (BPI). A letter come through informing us that we were looking at a 20 grand fine for our illegal piracy racket and all our tapes must be destroyed. I'd only just bought a gaff with my girlfriend at the time and had visions of those fuckers taking my flat, as I didn't have 20p to give 'em, never mind 20 large. As it was my address on the letter, my silent partner was a bit blasé about it all, which pissed me off no end. In the end, a good mate got me/us off the hook. I didn't ask how, but I was incredibly grateful for his intervention.

Man, I could see my relationship going down the toilet before I'd even learned how to use a lawnmower. I fucked it up the following year anyway. But that's another story...

Top
Greenwood First School, 1975
Greg Phillips - far right, middle row
Me - right, floor.

The Deabill Family
Killowen Avenue, Xmas 1979
Back row - Dad with the Amish
beard, Nan Vi & Grandad Fred
and my beautiful mum. My hair
stuck in the mid-70s and bad form
on the Fred Perry buttons.

Photo by my sister, Nicole, with
her present that year, a Polaroid
camera.

Wardy the Punk, Mark Lyall and Paddy McCann, The Green Box, Russell Road, 1983.

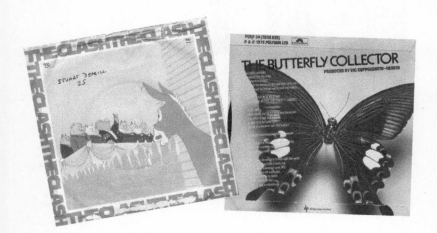

TO:
Stuart DEABILL
73 Gonville Crescent,
Northolt,
Middx.

L.T.E.

REFERENCE 025985

Costs due to

Driving Licence No. | Issued by | Different authority of residence

Sex | Date of Birth | Date of Conviction 19.12.83 | Date of Sentence (if different)

Offence	Offence Code	Date of Offence	Costs £ p	Fine £ p	Endorsements/Disqualification	Sentence Code
Rail fare fraud		30.9.83	15 00	35 00		

| | | | 15 00 | 35 00 | TOTAL DUE £ 50 00 | Time for Payment 7 days |

You were convicted on the date of hearing shown above by the MAGISTRATES' COURT sitting at the Court House, Green Lane, Ealing, and ordered so pay the sums shown

Payment should be made either by post to me, the Clerk to the justices, The Court House, Green Man Lane, Ealing, W.13, made personally at the same address between the hours of 9.30 a.m. and 12.00 noon and 2.00 p.m. and 4.00 p.m. Monday to y only

Failure to pay as ordered in paragraph 1 above will render you liable to arrest or your money and goods liable to distraint ut further notice, unless you have previously applied for and been granted further time to pay.

of further time to pay may be made either in person to the Court at 10.15 a.m. or by letter application is made.

R. B. GIDMAN
Clerk to the Justices.

ENTS.
be CROSSED and made payable to the CLERK TO THE JUSTICES.
stamped. Cash should be sent by registered post.

British Rail
Inter-City
Return

To Leeds City
194

Issued subject to the Regulations and
Conditions in the Publications and Notices
of the British Railways Board.
Not transferable

Price | Class

From

Ticket No. | Date

Outward

To pay is to fail – unless you get caught

2 TONE

2 TONE 45

GANGSTERS
THE SPECIAL A.K.A.

45

· MADNESS

MY GIRL ·

My only ever gig at the Oriel Youth Centre, Carr Road, Northolt, summer 1989.
Pure garageband vibe.

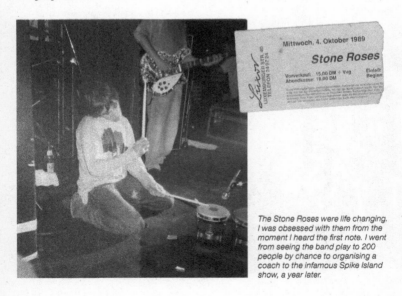

Mittwoch, 4. Oktober 1989

Stone Roses

Vorverkauf: 15,00 DM + Vvg.   Einlaß:
Abendkasse: 19,00 DM   Beginn

The Stone Roses were life changing.
I was obsessed with them from the
moment I heard the first note. I went
from seeing the band play to 200
people by chance to organising a
coach to the infamous Spike Island
show, a year later.

CHELSEA FOOTBALL CLUB
Member's Identity Card

SEASON 1984-85

Name: S DEABILL

No: 05648   Associate

ENGLAND TRAVEL CLUB

Name: S DEABILL
Expiry Date: 31. 12. 90
Membership no.: 6073

Chief Executive

THIS MEMBERSHIP CARD IS THE PROPERTY OF THE
ENGLAND TRAVEL CLUB, IN LANCASTER GATE, LONDON W2 3EW
AND IS NOT TRANSFERABLE

THE HOLDER OF THIS CARD AGREES TO ABIDE
BY THE RULES OF THE ENGLAND TRAVEL CLUB

Adult

ENGLAND

Card expires: 31.12.2000

S DEABILL
68290

MEMBERS
CLUB

CFC
CHELSEA FOOTBALL CLUB
Member's Identity Card
SEASON 1990/91

Name: S. DEABILL

No: 20145X

Chelsea and England.
I used to go to a lot of England games in the late 80's and early 90's, but struggled to write about them.
Mainly because so much happened off the pitch, it's probably better for all concerned the stories stay
in the pub rather than in print. Mad times.

My Ever Changing Moods
The Style Council

SJM CONCERTS presents
in association with

PRIMAL
SCREAM
SATURDAY 2nd APRIL 1994
8:00pm - 2:00am
Tickets £12.00
GLASGOW BARROWLANDS
244 GALLOWGATE, GLASGOW

01721

The Smiths

ASTORIA THEATRE
157, CHARING CROSS ROAD
LONDON WC1

METROPOLIS MUSIC
PRESENT

FLOWERED
U P
WITH GUESTS
THURSDAY 12th SEPTEMBER 1991
IT'S ON .... FROM 8.00pm TO 2.00am

£7.50   TICKET NO.
          00214

RIGHT OF ADMISSION RESERVED
TO BE RETAINED

SUBTERANIA   Tel 081 960 4590
12 ACKLAM ROAD LADBROKE GROVE   LONDON W10

THURSDAY 4 APRIL 1991 Doors 8.00pm - 2.00am

PAUL WELLER'S MOVEMENT

Admission £6.00   Ticket № 86

Ticket not valid without a counterfoil

The Lodgers

The Style Council were playing Brighton in June on a Saturday night. I didn't need asking twice. That English love affair with the seaside for the landlocked, like myself, Dizzy and Danny O'Connor (OK, the Irish as well), always made for a good weekend away. It would certainly be a lot less violent this time round, unlike the last time I was there, with Chelsea, 2 years previous.

We headed down to the coast for the night. No hotel booked but, back then, it was either a case of turning up at the local information office and letting them ring round to look for a basic B&B or walking around Regency Square seeing who still had vacancies.

We ended up getting a triple room in a rundown B&B on the square through the Aussie geezer on the desk. A quick shower, put on the finest clobber that one's wages would allow, and then head downstairs for a pre-gig sherbet. It wasn't long before we were half-pissed.

The Wombat behind the jump joined us for a few beers and was telling us about his time in Brighton. After a couple of drinks, the banter was in full flow. He told us that you could always tell who happened to be gay down there because the fellas wore bangles on their wrists. The further the bangle falls down the forearm, the more fist they can get up a partner's arsehole.
Strewth!

We pissed ourselves at this analogy, as teenagers do, and started checking the bar for well-groomed geezers with bangles just to be on the safe side (like any self-respecting gay gentleman would go anywhere near us three).

After a couple more beers, 'Skippy', as we'd taken to call him (ask your weird uncle, kids) disappeared to book some guests in and came back five minutes later with steam coming out of his ears, giving us evils.

I asked him what the problem was. He said that someone had nicked his wallet. Now, he was more pissed than us at this point and then he accuses us of theft, the cheeky fucker!

We all told him he was bang out of order and it started to get a bit heated. Skippy was on about calling the Old Bill but the other two decided it was time to leave before I started launching ashtrays at the twat. And the pubs were open now anyway.

By the time we got into The Centre, along with another 4,500 young 'Councillors', the atmosphere was electric. 'Our Favourite Shop' was at number 1 and the band were on fire. I saw the show a couple of days previously at a hot and sweaty Brixton Academy and blew the roof off. That mid-period Council was their peak for me in a live setting. Dee, Whitey, Micky T, PW, Camelle Hinds on bass, Helen Turner on keys, Stevie Sidelnyk on percussion and the brass team. Musicianship off the scale.

'When You Call Me', 'Internationalists', 'Long Hot Summer', 'A Stone's Throw Away' and 'Whole Point 2'. An amazing set with a big old finish of 'Walls Come Tumbling Down'. Unity is powerful!

DJ Gary Crowley was at the bar when we dipped out for yet another pint mid-set. Gary's Tuesday Club at our local venue, Bogarts, was legendary, and I was a big fan of his radio shows on Capital at the time.

Dizzy shouted at him (loudest geezer in the world with a beer in him): "GARY! GARY! DO YOU WANT A DRINK MATE?"

"Hi boys! No thanks. Some lovely women down here, don't you think?"
Dizzy: "OH FUCKING YEAH!"
Danny: "Where? I'm dying for a ride!"

Afterwards, we decided to head back to the B&B as I had trainers on, and we knew getting into a club would be a mare. I was buzzing from the gig and thought it could get on top with Skippy, but I was fucked if I was going to bed just yet. More booze needed!

We walked, no sorry, we fell into the bar and the Aussie was all over us like smallpox. "Boys! Boys! I'm so sorry! My wallet had fallen out of my pocket, under the bar, and I panicked. We got robbed here a while back. Let me buy you a few beers to say sorry and sort you out a bit of tucker". Apology accepted, beers had, sandwiches mullered and Skip has turned the music up as we merrily attempted to boogie round the hotel bar to the likes of Prince, The Rolling Stones and fucking INXS.

Unfortunately, by the time it had gone midnight, Dizzy could barely stand or see straight. We knew it was time to call it in when some brightly dressed flower walked in and Diz shouts over the bar to him: "MATE! HOW FAR UP DOES YOUR BANGLE GO?"

The lodgers were certainly in disgrace that night.

Egg and Chips

If Paul Weller or Stiff Little Fingers' Jake Burns made me want to play guitar, then Billy Bragg's brilliant debut, *Life's A Riot with Spy vs Spy*, told me I could do it. One man and his guitar. Before that, it was just something I felt was out of my grasp. I bought a cheap second-hand electric guitar from a dodgy old shop in South Harrow, run by a certifiable weirdo. I proceeded to drive myself, my nan, my grandad and the next-door neighbours mad for the next few weeks as I tried in vain to keep the strings down on the fretboard long enough to make a proper sound. The action was so far out, the strings seemed like they were in another postcode.

Luckily for everyone, I didn't have enough money for an amplifier at that point but plugged in through my Pioneer stereo. It soon occurred to me that plucking notes wouldn't get me far. After buying a chord book and working out how to play the intro to The Jam's 'All Mod Cons', and pissing about with different chord configurations around A, D and E, I got something resembling a rhythmic sound for at least five seconds.

But Johnny Marr? More like Johnny Morris from *Animal Magic*, hammering away trying to get my fingers into barre chord and F sharp shapes. Eventually, I learnt The Troggs, 'Wild Thing' and thought "This is the start of something!"

After a year or so with the finger-bleeding axe (I might as well have played a real fucking axe, the amount I cut myself), I upgraded to a Fender Tele copy. Around this time, I started jamming with a mate, Loz, and he was a natural. I thought I'd have a go at singing. Jesus! My vocals made my guitar playing look competent. I have a memory of attempting Easterhouse's debut single, 'Whistling in the Dark', in my nan's front room while she was out at Bingo. Loz wisely moved on and formed a band with stoner Marcus, Antony Poole on drums and Loz's brother, Fred, on vocals.

After much deliberation, I went out and bought an Epiphone Casino. Ideally, like most blokes of a certain age, I'd have loved to have bought a Rickenbacker 330 or 360, but they were well out of my price range. Weller played the Casino with The Style Council and, for me, it was nearly as iconic as the guitars he played with The Jam. 'Internationalists' from *Our Favourite Shop* was a real powerhouse of a tune, and I thought that if I could try and channel a tiny bit of that, fame and fortune weren't far away.

I was writing lyrics all the time, either about getting blown out by a bird, falling in love with a bird and then getting blown out, or it was some anti-Thatcher/Tory rant.

In 1988, both myself and Loz got some temp work in Kingsbury, working in the Granada TV Rentals warehouse. I'd also moved to Harrow where I made the mistake of sharing the gaff with Fred and his uptight bird, Lesley, who kept chinchillas. And she loved them more than Fred!

It was a short bus ride to work, where we had use of a ghetto blaster and would smash out our own mix tapes while loading vans for the drivers to deliver TVs to homes around the area. It didn't take me long to see a flaw in the system and exploit it. One of the newer drivers seemed to be on my wavelength and I used to add the odd brand-new Grundig or Matsui onto his van. He would deliver straight to a mate. Everything was paperwork back then, and there were over 500 TVs in the warehouse, so it was easy to 'forget' to mark all the stock. What I didn't know was that one of the other staff members was doing the same!

While I was working there, I met this older fella called Gary, who had been in bands and was interested in the songs I was writing. He asked me if I fancied doing something band-wise with him. I was flattered, so I went to his flat on the West Hendon Estate, which he shared with his missus, two young twins and a new-born, and thought, "Fucking hell! Is he bringing them on the road too?"

Over egg and chips, he told me his missus was the drummer. A proper Partridge Family set-up. In between the dinner, the kids rucking, his missus shouting and the baby crying, we sat down, and he taught me a few riffs and chord structures; songs that my basic palette could take in. Fair play to him. I wanted to learn The Stooges, 'I Wanna Be Your Dog', so he showed me how to play it but then said to do 'Let's Dance', the Chris Montez early-60s pop classic, which I hated. But somehow, we managed to put a few things together, and he gave me some homework. It was the first time I'd met someone who had a bit of talent on the guitar and was grateful he took an interest.

We reconvened a week later back at his gaff and we put some of my words to his tunes. By the fifth week, we had about ten songs including

'I Wanna Be Your Dog', 'Let's Dance' and the bleedin' 'Hippy Hippy Shake'! The next week was going to be the one where his wife would get behind the kit. Great! Proper amps, rehearsal room, the lot! When he said he was going to set up in his cramped front room, my heart sank.

After work, myself and Gary got the bus to his place, and he was excited about the night's session. As we arrived at his flat on the rundown estate, with my Epiphone in hand, and in the pissing rain, I just had that gut instinct that it was going to be too weird. I was grateful Gary had taken an interest, but my attention was more on what Loz's band was doing rather than this. Gary, bless him, was a big lad and the wrong side of 30. His missus scared me, and the kids weren't far behind! I went up and there wasn't room to swing their cat. We did two songs, had more of the kids rucking and even more of his missus shouting at Gary, plus Gary moaning at me that I was out of tune while the cat happily pissed on the carpet.

The baby slept through it. The egg and chips were nice though!

I made my exit and said to Gary, who looked broken, that I'd see him at work the next day, as he followed me down the stairs of the flats, apologising. Once I walked into the miserable evening, the good lady wife was straight out of the top-floor window shouting at him to get back upstairs and clean up the cat piss. I got the bus back to Harrow thinking "Fuck this! Time to move on".

The next day, Gary apologised again and said let's try again next week, and he'd get the missus and kids out of the way. I couldn't say no because he looked like he'd had a night of torture.

In the middle of all these rehearsals, he'd advertised for a bass player. Into the breach came Alex, this student-looking type. God help him. But, with the promise of Gary's family being absent, at least we could start to try and look like something resembling a band.

Imagine the surprise when I went to Gary's that week and was greeted by one of his kids at the door, holding a toy gun menacingly. Up the stairs, the usual chaos ensued and, sitting in the middle of it all, was this softly spoken geezer who'd just smashed a plate of egg and chips. Welcome to the club, mush!

We ran through a couple of numbers and the sound started to fatten out. Gary was so excited with the new line-up, he let out a massive fart and said - "Smell that, kids!" with an air of triumph. At least it covered the aroma of cat piss! Later that week, Gal approached me in the work office waving a letter as I was trying to chat up one of the girls and said, "We've cracked it! We've got an audition for *Opportunity Knocks* in three weeks' time!"

For those born in more recent years, *OK* was the *OG* of talent shows; *Britain's Got Talent* is a direct relative of the show.

I didn't know what to say. *Opportunity Knocks* might have made careers for groups like The Real Thing, but I was an edgy ex-casual who was just about to see any hard-earned credibility fly out of the office window, along with the chance of taking Sue from video rentals out for a Harvester and a hand shandy. I think Gary could sense my disappointment, as my face told no lies at the thought of being on one of Granada's new range of tellies that had just been delivered, and on a show that was Cringe Factor 10.

The next week's practice brought some real bad vibes off Gal's missus. "What's up with you, Stuart? Gary said you don't want to do this audition. After everything he's done for you, you miserable wanker!"

Gary, for once, didn't look embarrassed and I realised he felt exactly the same as her. I was now trapped by my own guilt. I said "OK, let's give it a go". Gary had entered a previous band he was in with this early Beatles-type tune, 'Shout About It', on cassette and it had taken six months to go through the due process, hence why we now had a crack at it. I didn't even know what the band was called but if it was as shit as the tune, then it wouldn't have surprised me if it was called 'Egg and Chips'.

When Alex was given the news, I think he felt as bewildered as I did with it all. I'm sure the advert said, "Bass player needed for an indie rock outfit", not a cabaret turnout. Gary and his missus were besides themselves with excitement and hired a local hall to have a production run-through. At least it didn't smell of cat piss. Gary had told us all to wear white shirts as we'd have to look smart for the audition, and wanted to treat this rehearsal, to a backing tape, as the real thing. The icing on the cake was him turning up with two ties for myself and Alex to put round our Gregory's. Red ties. I said, "No fucking way! And red?" He was Arsenal and knew full well who I supported.

Then his missus starts screaming from behind the kit. "You fackin' wear it, you moany ungrateful twat!" and she launched a drumstick at me. Like her drumming, well off and it hit the floor 5 metres away. I put down my guitar, seething, and steamed outside to get some air.

Gary followed and apologised for his wife's behaviour, although I could still hear her ranting away to Alex. He said not to worry about the tie and to just do the run-through. We had eight attempts of miming without any mics or stands with choreographed movements. I now knew what it was like to be in Milli Vanilli! I was so embarrassed by the whole thing that I didn't tell anyone what I was up to.

In the time between the letter landing and the audition, my contract ran out at Granada after an investigation into the missing TVs, VHS recorders and various other audio-visual paraphernalia that had gone awry. Luckily and unbeknown to me, Courtney, one of the other warehouse assistants, had been making a real dent in the stock, and he'd suddenly gone back to Jamaica, so all the questions were about whether we'd seen him up to no good. I pleaded ignorance while silently jumping inside because he was copping for what I'd had away, with the safety of him being 6,000 miles away.

Audition day arrived and, although I knew it was all wrong and I should have done the off when the gobby cow started launching sticks about at the rehearsal, my ego wouldn't let me. What if we won and got a summer season at Butlin's or Pontins? I'd be knee-deep in holiday crumpet and getting paid for it (I'd watched *That'll Be The Day* more than once). So, when I arrived at Riverside Studios in Hammersmith to meet the others, part of me thought this could be the start of something. I was still struggling on the guitar to play anything other than chords, but I'd at least learnt how to play rhythm, and to keep in time with the others.

We were shown to the dressing room by one of the production crew, to be confronted by all sorts of lunacy. A one-legged magician, three sisters dressed in gold lame singing 'There Must Be an Angel' at a pitch so high, it wouldn't have surprised me if it didn't set nearby Battersea Dogs Home into a frenzy, and this horrific Bonnie Langford-type screaming at her drama teacher to fetch her some Lilt because she couldn't tap dance without it.

What felt like an hour passed before we get the call to go up and perform. Gary made us wear the red ties and we looked like a fucking dog's dinner. His missus had really pushed the boat out and wore a red bowtie along with her oversized shirt and suit jacket. She was a short, wiry thing and looked like she was about to take off with boiling tension and excitement. We walked onto the stage looking like a collection of freaks. There's Gary, bulging out of his ill-fitting suit with a Darby the size of a Michelin tyre, Alex in his office suit with trousers that were far too long for his short legs, me in a navy blazer and black 501 jeans, which is a fashion faux pas anyway, and wifey behind the kit looking like Roland the Rat in a dickie bow!

One of the production crew counted us in and turned the cassette on, the PA blaring out the intro to 'Shout About It'. The vocals were live, and I purposely let Gary sing everything and chipped in with 'Shout About It' when it mattered. Gary was in his element. He loved being in a band and writing music. He was a nice fella, but somehow his career had been interrupted by Rat Girl. He told me he'd been in a Mod Revival band in '79, signed to Decca for a one-off single, and he was forever chasing his tail since that early brush of lower league fame on a major (but dying) label.

Unlike other shows, the team at *Opportunity Knocks* asks you back for a second audition within 10 minutes of coming off stage. Gary was convinced we would get through. I thought, "We've got to be better entertainment than those three sisters causing GBH of the earhole". Fifteen minutes passed. Gary couldn't take anymore and went and barged his way into an office down the hall to find out, partly due to Ratty driving him and us mad.

"Go and fackin' find out Gal, will ya?"

The slow walk back, and the life fully flushed from his big, round red mush, said it all. "We weren't what they were looking for".

Rat wanted to kick someone's head in, but I just wanted out. The one-legged magician was freaking me out, hobbling about the gaff with his poor caged rabbit.

We packed our gear up and I said, "Come on. Let's go and have a pint". After a couple of beers, and with Ratty banging on about getting back for the kids, Gary drained his pint and told me in that passive-aggressive way that it wasn't working, and that he was splitting the band, and skulked off with his wife. I feigned a degree of care, passed him his skinny red tie back and wished him well.

Myself and Alex stayed in the pub and got hammered. And that was the last I saw of Gary, his wife, the kids and the pissy cat. And I don't think I've eaten egg and chips since.

Made of Stone

The future comes for you, or to you, in many ways. A seismic moment that alters your course of thinking and being in an instant. It could be a death, a birth, a goal or, in this case, a bassline. Since the demise of The Smiths, I was buying a lot of records by the 'next big thing' guided by the *NME*, my weekly bible. The House of Love were amazing sonically, but lyrically it was largely introspective nonsense. Or take The Wedding Present; a bunch of student hobos banging on about lost love at 100mph just didn't do it for me. I wasn't a student and always dressed up for a night out, not down.

Others, like That Petrol Emotion and The Railway Children, were great, but I felt a bit lost believing in bands by the end of 1988. New groups just didn't have the swagger, the look, the songs or the attitude of wanting to change the world.

I'd gone to see The Wonder Stuff at The Astoria and they had some of the above but when the singer, Miles Hunt, started calling the audience cunts, maybe jokingly, I thought "Why would I pay money to be called a cunt? - I can go down the pub and get called that for free!" Maybe I'd been spoilt with former passions.

I was also desperate to become something more than a fan of music, at that point, but every time I got involved in a band, either managing or playing, it was a fucking disaster. So, when I least expected it, on a damp March night in North London, The Stone Roses stopped my world.

The future was mine.

I'd gone to the gig with my sister, Nicole, and my regular gig-going mate, Al. Nicole was friends with the guitarist of the support band, The Hollow Men. Brian had previously been in The Passmore Sisters, a lively, interesting four-piece from the North West who had recently split up after a drunken gig at ULU, where the drummer kicked over his kit and tried to attack one of the other band members. The Hollow Men didn't impress, and I was thinking about calling it a night when all these Mancs came in, bringing with them a football supporter vibe. Much different to the usual 'Student Grants' in de rigeur all-black double denim and stripy Breton tops.

I thought that if a load of Northerners had made the trip down, there must be something in it and I should give it a chance. I'd read a live review by Bob Stanley (soon to be of St Etienne) in *Melody Maker* a couple of weeks previously that was positive, but that was as much as I knew about the band.

The moment Gary 'Mani' Mounfield stroked the strings of his Rickenbacker bass guitar at The Powerhaus in Islington on March 15th, 1989, for the opening bars of 'I Wanna Be Adored', magic happened. I was transfixed. The singer, Ian Brown, stalked the stage like a tiger looking for its dinner. Alan 'Reni' Wren hunched over his cymbals, spraying out a groove with the sort of tension that was usually the domain of stadium bands. Guitarist John Squire, dropping liquid lines over a thin veil of FX, had my eyes and ears totally lost in the moment.

The group's travelling fans added to the atmosphere while dry ice filled the stage. When the drums kicked in, I was with the Mancs, lost in time and floating along. After all the *C86* and floppy haired non-ambitious white boy scratchy rock cobblers of the previous couple of years, here was a band with intent.

And there's no finer song than 'Adored' to reverse that trend.

By the time the Roses finished their exquisite hour-long set with a mind-blowing ten-minute 'I Am The Resurrection', nothing seemed the same. Every song they played was a winner. This was a band that looked at the stars, not their feet, and they had swing, bite and melodies to hang your hat on with a true sense of purpose.

They looked great and the front man owned the stage. More importantly, they had the songs and a groove.

Ian Brown, Alan 'Reni' Wren and John Squire, dressed in colourful long-sleeved tops and semi-flared jeans, looked like a gang, as all the best bands do. I came out of the half-full venue bouncing, wanting to tell the world what I'd just seen.

Al and I knew we had to see them again as quickly as possible. The following month, the band played Brunel University down the road in Uxbridge. It was an even better show, and we were left in no doubt that we were witnessing a group that would soon be playing the big gaffs, like Brixton Academy, The Brighton Centre or Manchester Apollo. We had no idea they would bypass the 3 to 4,000 capacity concert halls and play

the much larger Alexandra Palace inside the space of six months.
I suspect they didn't either.

A week later, the self-titled debut album was released, and it wasn't
received with the acclaim it deserved. The obsession went up tenfold
at my end as I played the album every day for the next six months. I
sought out former single releases such as 'Elephant Stone' and 'Sally
Cinnamon', and I felt the urge to let as many people as possible know that
The Stone Roses were the greatest band they'd never seen.

The *NME* reviewers didn't get it but, after the second Summer of Love
and the rave scene going off in a big way, the whole landscape changed.
The band's debut was a record for going out or coming down to. It was the
perfect foil for the E Generation. The magnificent 'Made of Stone' and
the chiming positivity of 'Waterfall', followed by its cousin, the backward
looping 'Don't Stop', the anthemic 'This Is the One', and the piercing soft
shuffle of 'Shoot You Down' gave the soundtrack to a ground-breaking
record of their very own for the counter-culture revolution sweeping
the nation.

I saw the band another couple of times, at London's ICA and Bristol's
Bier Keller before they regrouped and realigned for the next phase. The
weekly music press went mental for them, and they were cover stars on
Sounds, *Melody Maker* and *NME* by August.

By the autumn of 1989, The Stone Roses had accumulated fans far
and wide.

When I found out the band was booked to play a tour in Europe in October, I had to go. The furthest I'd been to a gig at that point was Dublin, to see The Smiths, so I was gagging to go further afield. I had the dough to back up the trip and I got a week off work to follow the dream. The only snag was that none of my mates were able to afford it, could get the time off work or wanted to accompany me. As much as I didn't mind my own company and occasionally went to football on my tod, I didn't fancy a few days away on my own.

As the gigs got nearer, I spotted a small ad in *NME*: "Male looking for like-minded fans of The Stone Roses to accompany him to watch the group in Europe".
Wow! Somebody else gets it!

However, being acutely aware that this could be some sort of nut-nut or a wrong un, I got Nicole to check him out. After a phone conversation, my sister told me he sounded OK, and that Simon Kelly worked at the Royal Albert Hall box office. My eyes and ears lit up. I suddenly saw the possibility of front-row gigs!

We set up a meet at his workplace and went for a pint, talking excitedly about the music we were into and the upcoming Roses tour. I came away thinking he was a bit different but OK, and that I wasn't going to get touched up or knifed in my sleep.

We arranged the gigs we wanted to go to and booked a flight out to Hamburg for the first one. This was going to be followed by shows in

Cologne, Amsterdam and Paris over the course of five days.

As we landed in Hamburg, Simon suggested that we head to the venue to have a look and to see if anyone was about. Simon was less reserved than me when it came to meeting bands. I still considered certain artists as stars and treated them accordingly if they were in the vicinity. He remarked that he'd met the Roses backstage before at a gig in Oxford.

After locating the Logo Club and pushing open a massive door, we were greeted by the band, who had just finished their soundcheck. John Squire ushered us in after our polite request to join them. I was inwardly ecstatic! Over the PA came two songs that sounded like The Roses but weren't familiar. The second track was a monster, and longer than 'I Am The Resurrection'. With its funky breakbeat, hypnotic bassline and funked up wah-wah guitar, I was totally entranced by it. Mani bowled over excitedly and asked us, "What do you think of the new single, lads?" We had just heard 'Fools Gold' and 'What The World Is Waiting For' for the first time. I was that gobsmacked, I just blurted out "Fackin' brilliant!"

By the time the gig came around, I was flagging, even though I had a couple of beers inside me. That soon changed once the band came on, and I spent the whole gig standing on a chair, shuffling along. There couldn't have been more than 200 in the venue that night.

In Simon's words: "We stayed on after the gig, where we met up with a crazy English girl who put us up for the night. She was very proud of the fact that she'd let Clint Boon sign her tit when the Inspiral Carpets were

WEST SIDE STORIES - NOTES FROM NORTHOLT

over. We had a nervous sleep in her flat that night".

We woke up the next day and made our way by train to Cologne. The weather was decent, and we found a great hotel where we could finally chill out and grab a snooze. It was my first time in the city, and I was a bit taken aback that hardly anyone spoke English. I wasn't impressed. Yes. I'm aware of my own shallow shortcomings now. Simon was a bit horrified by my "two world wars" comments every time I asked somebody something and got a curt reply in their native tongue.

The gig itself was inside a smaller venue than The Logo, but it was busy, and the crowd was a bit livelier than the previous night. After three songs, the locals started chanting at the band, which seemed to get under Ian's skin. He said something cutting, which I picked up on after the gig with him as we felt confident enough to go backstage without being told to fuck off. There were a few other English bods on the tour, as well as a Japanese girl. "A few ignorant Germans in tonight, Ian". An instant retort of "A few ignorant English in tonight, lad" certainly put me in my place.

The night ended with the Roses dancer/FX master and birthday boy, Cressa, being wheeled out of the venue on a trolley because he was mullered on brandy and spliff.
How we laughed!

It was inner sanctum stuff, but God forbid thinking that you were a part of it all. Those four, and their crew, were very much an impenetrable Mancunian gang. All the best bands have that. Their own language, humour and barrier. They reminded me of The Clash in that each member was equal to the sum of their parts.

The next night was a gig at the Amsterdam Milkveg. The Dam. The Promised Land. The freedom, the drugs and the shop windows. Every schoolboy's dream city break. It was Simon's first time in the city, and I took great delight in showing him The Bulldog Palace and other such relaxed premises once we found a cheap hotel for the night. And, as we did in Hamburg, we turned up at the venue for soundcheck and walked straight in. The Milkveg was bigger than the previous nights' venue and it had a proper feel to it. The magic was certainly in the air.

I shared a spliff with Ian as he shuffled along to Reni's amazing drumming, which seemed to go on forever. Ian took the spliff off me, drew in a big puff and announced excitedly, "It's alright here in the Dam, innit?!"

The gig itself was a blur. Too much herb, but we went backstage afterwards anyway. The band were relatively calm after slaying the audience with a well-honed set. Even the B-sides were amazing live. 'Mersey Paradise', 'Where Angels Play' and especially 'Standing Here', for me, were head and shoulders above the rest. Only fellow Mancunians Happy Mondays were on any sort of parity at this point.

As I badly rolled another spliff, Reni was shouting: "Anyone got any herb?" repeatedly. I pulled myself off the floor where I was sitting spaced out and handed him the joint. He looked at me and said,

"Don't make a meal of it, lad".

And that was my cue to see that we'd overstayed our welcome. Simon stayed chasing a bit of skirt, but I went back to the hotel to get some well-needed kip, even if the room was spinning violently.

Paris. The last gig of the tour was the biggest to date and one where it was very much "Manchestoh vibes in the area". There was a big northern presence in and around La Cigalle that night and, with Felt and The La's (who really lit up the room) supporting, it had the makings of yet another monumental show.

The Roses came on to their intro track with a piercing siren loop and the gaff erupted. I don't think the Parisians, all leather jackets and drainpipes, knew what had hit them.

"Manchestoh! La La La! Manchestoh! La La La!"

Simon and I stayed on the balcony to watch the band. We were both still knackered from the night before and spending a week together had started to grate, especially as we were relying on one of his pals for a kip for the night. I was grumpy. I've never been a fan of Paris. I'd been over the year before when myself, Lock and a neighbour, Mick Mabbs, got a Euro Rail Pass and were city-hopping around France, The Netherlands, Germany and Italy. We'd done the sightseeing stuff in Paris back then and I was left feeling bored shitless.

And the locals always let you know what they think of the English as well!

Our trip to Pere Lachaise Cemetery, to see Jim Morrison's grave, was an eye-opener. I was going through a Doors phase and the cult of the dead rock star seemed to be in the ascendancy, especially once Oliver Stone's The Doors movie had put Jim, Robby, John and Ray back in the public eye some 17 years on from Jim's mysterious death.

As we walked up the hill, there were some people hanging round the grave, with one kid lying across it without a single fuck given. I thought "Where's the respect in that, you little twat?" I told the fucker so and walked back down the hill as quickly as I'd walked up it. I think he'd taken the song 'Break on Through' a bit too literally!

Anyway, back in the room and that unique putrid smell that can only be CS gas started to fill my senses during the second song, bringing tears to most people's eyes. I somehow have a high tolerance to it, as I'd found out the following year at an England away game when all my mates went down choking but I was still on high alert.

The group tried to get into the classic 'Made of Stone' before Brownie led the band off stage to try and bring some order to proceedings, and to let the fumes clear. Hopefully, the soppy cunt with the can of CS gas would be dealt with.

On the Roses' debut album sleeve is a lemon, which apparently negates the effects of the gas. In the Paris Riots of 1968, some of the rioters would be sucking on a lemon while giving the local Gendarme, what for. Ian, especially, was taken with this. That night in Paris, it was either somebody making a historical gesture on behalf of John Squire's fantastic artwork, or a pissed northerner who'd been shopping that afternoon and bought the cannister to let off 'for a laugh'.

Once the gig got back under way, the intensity of the performance went up a notch and the band showed exactly why they were worth following. Afterwards, when we'd finally found our way back to Simon's friend's apartment, I was too knackered for small talk, especially as I couldn't speak a word of French apart from *'Oui'* (being the ignorant English-abroad fuck that I was). After a rough night's sleep, we got the train back to Calais to board the homeward-bound boat.

At the port, I bumped into John Squire, the quietest Roses member. He nodded an acknowledgement my way as I said, "Brilliant gigs, John!".
He smiled and disappeared into the sea mist, as any self-respecting guitar hero should.

Energy Flash

Little fellas. Jack and Jills. Smarties.

All in the name of Ecstasy, the wonder drug that took back-bedroom potheads, young shop workers, high-flying city bods, hairdressers, mechanics, grafters, students, villains and hooligans, and made everyone equal. The new religion. The clubs became churches, the DJs became the new messiahs, and the doormen were still moody fuckers, but the UK had become one big dancefloor.
And Northolt was no exception.

My own personal journey into this brave new world came via one of the locals in The Swan - 'Wee-Wee' as he was known. God knows why. He wasn't short and he didn't piss himself (to my knowledge).

But, before I took on the talk of the town, I was in a rehearsal room off The Target Roundabout with Loz, Fred and Joe, trying to work out how to play Guns and fucking Roses, 'Sweet Child O' Mine' on rhythm guitar, when our drummer, Ant, walks in from yet another late night in his usual unshaven, dishevelled but happy state.

"Where did you go last night, Ant?"
"The Trip at The Astoria"
"Fucking Hippy"
"Bwahahaha! You ain't got a clue, Stu. It's amazing!" And then he sat behind the kit and bashed out a rhythm and away we went.

Loz was the only one who had any real ability, though Fred was a decent frontman and Joe still plays with bands to this day. Loz was the main man for arranging, playing and knocking a tune out. I was just someone that wanted to be on stage desperately and 'to be someone'. I had no real quality other than writing lyrics, and they were usually either oblique stoned cobblers or about another bird that blew me out. Anyway, after half an hour, Ant would be sweating out last night's toxins and the beat became more erratic than the bus timetable for the 140.

As we went outside for a smoke, I asked him what 'The Trip' was all about. I knew about acid house, of course, but being older than most of the lads down the pub who had started wearing ponchos, wallabees and beads, it passed me by immediately. Anything stronger than a bit of Lebanese hash scared the fuck out of me, almost as much as those bright orange Global Hypercolour tee shirts, visible from Mars, that had become part of the look.

I'd seen one of my younger mates, Steve, lose the plot on acid and he was never the same after. A gifted young footballer, he got bored at 14 with playing five days a week, be it with school, a local club, our district, the borough and, eventually, Watford. He sacked off the silky skills for booze and The Beatles. Eventually (in his mind) he morphed into Lennon and shouted out refrains from long-lost interviews by the protagonist.

"Everything will be OK in the end. If it's not OK, it's not the end, Stu!"
"Nobody controls me. I'm uncontrollable!"

Quite!

Anyway, one day, a mutual friend tells me Steve is lost down the microdot tunnel and quoting The Maharishi, Arthur Daley and Syd Barratt wearing Jesus boots and shit jeans. He was never the same again, bless him, and that put me right off those tiny bits of mind-altering coloured paper.

"So, what happens at these do's then, mate?"
"Well, it's like a mad carnival. It's all about the music and lights and E. You know that track I played you? 'Jesus on the Payroll' by Thrashing Doves?
(Yeah, I did. I loved it, but he also played me a load of bleeps and whistles that sounded like outtakes of 'One Man and His Dog' on a loop).
"Well, its eight hours of stuff like that and goes on 'til 6am".
(To my mind, that's mental. I struggle with anything past 2am and, by that time, I'd be pissed, thrown up twice and usually upset either one of my mates, the bouncers or a bird in the club).

"So, this E. What does it do?"
"I dunno! It's a bit like a warm bath, a decent shag and your team winning the FA Cup all at once. And everyone who's on it feels the same. Everyone is really happy!"

"Fuck me! That sounds mental mate. Still fucking hippie bollocks though, innit!"
"Hahahahaha! You should come, mate. Get a smiley tee shirt and get on one!"

It definitely appealed, but no way was I taking a fucking pill that felt like having a bath and then dancing to some cunt whistling all night.

He was a top lad, Ant. Cool, funny and didn't give a shit about much. We went back in and carried on rehearsing the set for our upcoming debut gig at Oriel Youth Centre on Carr Road.
Which brings me to Wee-Wee.

We're in The Swan one Saturday night and there's talk of a small rave-type party in Perivale, next to the Grand Union Canal. The bloke running it is a rave DJ and he's got a decent sound system in.

Anyway, Wee-Wee convinces a few of us to go and he's got some E for sale. I tell myself "Right! Let's have a go and see what it's all about" We get a cab, which takes about 15 minutes. We pull up by the lock and I look for a warehouse or an industrial building. Instead, there's music pumping from a small house.

I say to Wee-Wee: "Is this the gaff?"
"Yeah. It'll be mobbed though. Loads coming over from Wembley and Harrow"

I walk in and there's only five people there, sitting down whilst Justin the DJ is 'in the mix'. Head down and nodding in unison to some house track. He bounces over.
"Alright lads! Loads coming. Still early. Put your beers in the kitchen and don't drop any cherries on the carpet".

A few of the girls from The Swan turn up in the next cab, pissed, and start demanding Luther Vandross.

I'm starting to debate if this is the right atmosphere to drop my first pill. Anyway, Wee-Wee asks if I want to buy anything and I say to just give me a quarter of one.

"A quarter? Fuck off! Tell you what. He wants half a pill over there (points at a pony-tailed geezer in semi-flares with buck teeth, a Harrow bod). I'll split it between you both".
"OK!"

I take the half, have a nibble, put the remainder in my pocket and wait. And wait. And wait.

The music seems louder, but this is shit. The birds are falling over each other, drinking Thunderbird, the DJ's bass is in your face, but not in a good way, and Wee-Wee is dribbling.

I bail out with my mate, Richie, and get a cab home. I get indoors, make a cup of tea and empty my pockets of loose change then see the remaining bit of pill.

I feel quite mellow and roll a spliff, then let the harsh-tasting chalky texture of the E sit on my tongue for a nano-second and swallow it with the tea. (I have an asbestos mouth).

Thirty minutes later, I start to sweat. I feel very weird but also strangely hyper. I decide to take Ben the dog out for a walk. The Jack Russell looks at me as if to say, "Are you fucking nuts?", but wags his tail anyway.

Then I start to rush as the cold air hits me. I start telling the dog it's my best mate. I see a couple staggering up the road as I bounce down it. "Hiya! Good night? Where you been? Lovely weather innit?"

You can see the fear in their eyes, but they laugh nervously all the same as their stagger suddenly becomes a sprint.

I then decide to walk back to the house and have this urge to listen to Happy Mondays to see if there are any coded messages for this sudden euphoria. I drink a pint of water because I'd read you need to keep hydrated when rushing. Jack scuttles off to his bed.

Time slipped away watching *Night Network* and eventually, after pacing about for what seemed like an eternity, I finally get into bed. Even though I'm knackered, sleep is suddenly evasive. There are sparks fizzing as I close my eyes and I suddenly feel the urge to knock one out. And that becomes a fruitless task! What is this? I'm done with this weirdness. Wait till I see Wee-Wee.

I wake up the next morning feeling OK, a bit dazed and slightly wired but certainly better than last week's hangover after a late one in The Swan.

By the time I get to see Wee-Wee again, I'm thinking "Let's try another one" as I'm going to see The Stone Roses at Ally Pally.

Now that was where the full-on Ecstasy experience made sense, even if they didn't, in a venue too big and with a PA too small. But none of this really mattered. My crew were on one, loving the world and rushing so hard, it was like being in the middle of new beginnings; a new landscape and a cavalcade of talking absolute bollocks to anyone who would listen.

It paved the way for the next decade and some of the nights of our lives.

Glastonbury 90

There's a certain kind of magic that Glastonbury incites, which makes it a unique and fantastic experience for nearly all who visit. The site at Worthy Farm is sandwiched between the villages of Pilton and Pylle, with Glastonbury Tor overseeing what constitutes an area the size of Oxford. You can really feel the energy that the ancient ley lines bring, which I know sounds like mad old hippie bollocks but there's something different in the air before you've necked a Jack and Jill.

It's unlike anything else I've been to before or since. I've been 4 times, in 1990, 1994, 1995 and, for six hours, in 1997. 94 and 95 were brilliant. The line-ups were much more to my taste with great weather both times. I'd also got my nut round the site and its many fields, making it pay for itself by serving up. 1997 was the year the farm became a 6-mile-long quagmire with torrential rain in the run-up and across the weekend. My then-girlfriend hated every second of being onsite, and although I was desperate to see Primal Scream play the Friday night, her moaning won. We retreated and my wheel-spinning motor had to be towed off the site without us seeing a single note played.

The festival is now such an important part of the music calendar. Its varied performing arts set-up means there's something for everyone, with open arms to all forms of popular culture. The amount of BBC TV and radio coverage Glastonbury gets has helped catapult the festival's global standing. What Michael Eavis, wife Joan and, in more recent times, his daughter Emily have created since the festival's humble beginnings in 1970 is nothing short of beautiful, brilliant, eccentric and revolutionary.

It's gone from a hippie hang out with a pre-rock-God Marc Bolan to a global phenomenon, where most artists would sell their own grannies to be involved.

A couple of my mates had gone to previous festivals, and as much as I loved getting pissed, stoned and listening to some of my favourite bands in the open air, it was offset against the thought of camping, general outdoor living and shitting into a pit through a shared wooden khazi. Not my idea of fun, even less so for those unfortunate enough to fall into it. At least at Reading Festival you could just go for the day. It was close enough to home to do the off after the headliner.

I was off work sick with a broken finger thanks to a plastic Paddy breaking two of his teeth on my fist during the World Cup game against the Republic. I somehow managed to make it work in my favour by going into work the following day and pretending to pull the van door shutter down onto my wounded hand. Because I had a witness (poor old John, who wasn't happy I was about to leave him with an agency bod as a driver's mate for the next two weeks), London Linen had to give me full wages once I'd delivered the doctor's note. She wasn't having it that I'd done it at work but signed me off anyway. Happy days!

After a few days off at home and immersing myself in the football, I'd got that Friday feeling a bit early and popped into The Swan for a lunchtime jar where two regulars, Karen and Michelle, were talking about going to Glastonbury.

All the local hoods, dealers and loons had set off on Wednesday to get a decent camping spot to congregate on, but also to use the place as a base to serve up puff, acid and E. The girls started doing a number on me and said I should take them. I'd thought about going before, but most of my mates were football and it was a miracle if you could get them to go to a gig, never mind a festival. I'd got off with Michelle a couple of times after the pub closed and, leading with my carnal lust rather than my unadventurous previous, I decided to go.

I shot home quickly, grabbed the old man's fishing tent that had sat unused for years, a sleeping bag, a few bags of crisps and some Moroccan hash, and I picked the girls up from the pub. While I was grabbing the tent, they had ponced a pound off all the old boys and pissheads, and they'd managed to scrape 30 quid together. We filled the Ford Escort MK4 up in the Esso garage next door and were away!

After a tedious four-hour stop/start drive down the M4 and A361 with the usual Friday traffic, and after following the many handmade road signs through the increasingly narrow lanes, we arrived at the site. Luckily for us most arrivals were already in so the queue for the car park was minimal. Now, we knew that everyone bunked in. No-one I knew apart from Al the Plod had ever bought tickets.
To pay is to fail.

What I didn't cater for was the car park being marshalled and tickets being checked. I thought you just rocked up, parked up and jibbed over the fence.

When the steward asked us where our tickets were, I blurted out "Oh! They're at the ticket office, mate. We just need to collect them"

Luckily, the steward was less Showsec bouncer and more Swampy the tree botherer. He seemed to be in his own world/foliage.

"OK man" pointing to some spaces 20 yards away while exhaling a big plume of ganja smoke. "Just park up over there for the minute (takes another bang on the reefer) and collect your tickets".

As soon as he turned back round, I drove past to where he gestured to leave the car and carried on driving while the girls cheered, laughing at the liberty of it all. Once we'd parked out of sight, we got the camping gear and bags out of the car and walked towards the site fence, hoping our entry into the festival would be just as fortuitous. As we excitedly approached the fence, we saw a group of around 10 to 12 people huddled round a bloke. On closer inspection, he was charging people to go under the fence as he'd dug a ditch out. We asked him if he could get us in and, because he took a fancy to Michelle, he let us all go in for free, hoping she'd hang about for a bang on his chalice. I think that's what he said anyway. Once we'd gone under the makeshift fence, the three of us quickly hurried our step and were away.
Buzzing!

What none of us were prepared for was the size of the gaff. I'd been to Reading Festival the previous year and was expecting a more ordered, evenly set-out site. Glastonbury though was beyond anything as

111

structured as that. It was like walking into a sprawling village suspended in its own timeframe. Because dusk was approaching, the onus was on us to find a space to pitch the tent and quickly get among it. And, more importantly, to get right on it.

After much fucking about, I finally got the tent up and wondered why it had suddenly gone quiet. The girls had fucked off without me! It suddenly dawned on me that I'm in the middle of a field, in the middle of a festival, on me tod.
Slags!

I downed a can of lager I'd been given by a neighbouring tent dweller and headed towards the Pyramid Stage. After a 15-minute walk heading towards where the most noise was coming from and passing through the busy stall area, where the famous Joe Bananas stands, I bumped into one of the Northolt lads, and he pointed me in the direction of the 'camp', a short walk up a mud track. It always amazes me how, in a place that had at any one point of time more than 200,000 people attending, I still managed to bump into people I knew. Like I say, it was a magic gaff.

As expected, the group of tents had been ringed off and it started to look like a scene from *Apocalypse Now*. Some of the group seemed pleased to see me and said hello and smiled. Some gurned, and some were dancing to the small beatbox playing techno. A couple of bods were on the way back down, looking a tad haunted and paranoid.

Still, it was good to see familiar faces even if they were on different warp factors. Then, out of one of the tents, Michelle and Karen appeared, tripping off their noggins and falling over each other laughing and generally taking the piss out of everyone, including me.

I'd got the hump by now and I asked one of the more sober lads if he fancied going to see Happy Mondays, who were due on at the Pyramid Stage. We were soon away from the increasing level of carnage.

The Mondays were one of the bands of the moment. The whole Madchester thing had caught alight among working-class kids as well as the students. The entire vibe was based on chaos, dance beats, guitars and the poetry of their singer, Shaun William Ryder. Alongside him, the one and only Bez, the shambolic shaman mesmerised with his maracas and unique shapes. I loved 'em. Their second album *Bummed*, and the subsequent singles and EPs, were superb and captured those extraordinary times perfectly.

However, after a few numbers, it was clear it just wasn't happening. The buzz of their entry and first track had subsided, the sound wasn't great, and it was pretty obvious that some of the band had gone early, judging by the state of them. The crowd around me didn't seem to mind too much as the light show was doing it for them. I'm not sure how significant E had become among the Glastonbury crowd at this point, but you could have lit up Paris on the Ready Brek glow coming off those tripping in the immediate area.

After watching the band I headed back to the camp to have a spliff and a beer. Unfortunately, it looked a bit moody, with stewards surrounding the tents, so fuck knows what had happened. Although drug taking was more or less given a free reign at Glastonbury, it wasn't quite cricket to openly serve up, and I can imagine the blatant dealing had come to their attention.

I walked straight on and went to find my tent. Luckily, I'd made a mental note of a big tee-pee job near to my abode with a skull-and-crossbones flag flying proudly above. I couldn't imagine the two girls would be returning anytime soon, if at all, and got my nut down. With the various noises floating about – stilted conversations, distant ghetto blasters house mixtapes belting out and some cunt strumming an acoustic guitar – it made for a tricky kip but, somehow, I eventually drifted off.

I was awake again by about 8am, still on my Jack but feeling good about the day ahead. I was well up for having a proper mooch about and seeing what else made up this mad carnival. The weather was decent as well.

It wasn't long before I saw Fred, Rory and a couple of other mates, and we grabbed some food. All the talk was of the night before and which artists were good, which stages everybody went to and who got wankered. The whole shebang! It wasn't too long before someone rolled a spliff. Soon, it was all silly laughter and craving for a burrito off the sort with the big lils in the food van opposite. After a while, we drifted towards the Pyramid Stage again to see what was happening, and the first band on were Boo Yah Tribe, a great Samoan hip-hop outfit from the States.

After a while of dawdling and smoking from field to field, from stage to stage, from Sensi to Leb, I decided to go back to the tent for a late afternoon snooze. On arrival, I was surprised to see Michelle and Karen, and they were very unhappy. So was I after they told me the tent had been robbed. Bags rifled, clothes nicked and even the straightening tongs gone! I don't know what was more mystifying; Karen thinking she was going to be able to plug in her tongs or some dirty bastard walking about with them.

After a half hour of general swearing and blaming each other, I got back on the booze and spliff, and the girls dropped another couple of tabs. Acid wasn't for me. It wasn't the right environment to do an E either. I couldn't be standing in a muddy field trying to cuddle strangers to The Cure.

And that's all I remember from the Saturday night. On Sunday morning, it had started raining again and I thought "Fuck this! I've had enough" Michelle had disappeared again, this time with a bloke. Karen was holed up in Camp Northolt, and a favourite tee of mine had been robbed, I felt dirty and crusty, and I'd heard Adamski's 'Killer' so many times I was repeating "So you want to be free" repeatedly to no-one in particular.

I packed up what was left of mine and went and found Karen to tell her I was off. She was so spaced, she just giggled. I told her all her gear was in the tent and asked her to bring it back. On the way to the car park, I saw Rory, Paul, Richie, Fred and Loz sitting amongst the trees. Apart from Fred, who was always lively, the rest looked like ghosts. The trips

115

had taken them to the edge. I said I was going if anyone wanted a lift back. Two of the lads mumbled, and two more said yes but stayed rooted to the tree.

Fred, bless him, took one look at the rest of them and said "Yeah! Let's fuck off. I can't be having this lot any longer", and we set off back to Northolt.

Hurry Up Harry

Harry from Stoke became landlord of my local pub, The Swan, in 1993. He was a strange charmless fella with a degree in bullshit and upsetting people, most of the time unknowingly. He just had this thing of opening his mouth and annoying the shit out of nearly everyone who met him. He was the first permanent landlord The Swan had seen since 'Scouse' left a couple of years previously. There'd been temporary managers, but most bailed out as it wasn't the easiest gaff to run. The Swan became the local drug drive-thru around the turn of the 90s. As the boozer had two entry points from Petts Hill, motors would pull in off the road at speed, stop, and a small-time dealer would rush to serve a customer. Within ten seconds, they were back on the road and away, off to get stoned or nutted, or both.

Ronald McDonald - eat your heart out, son!

Every now and then, the pub would get raided by the filth but somehow, everyone knew they were coming. God knows who was getting the tip-off, but everybody carrying would hide their gear or just go home and have a rare night off. By the time the same old faces from Harrow or Ealing nick turned up and told everyone to get on the floor, there was nothing to be had other than a bit of resin found deep in a jean pocket that had been overlooked by said holder.

This happened every 6 months and the only arrest they usually made was of my mate, Grayzie. He loved to sing the old terrace favourite about the infamous triple cop killer, Harry Roberts, every time the Old Bill turned up.

"HARRY ROBERTS IS OUR FRIEND, IS OUR FRIEND, IS OUR FRIEND. HARRY ROBERTS IS OUR FRIEND. HE KILLS COPPERS!"

Unfortunately, Grayzie, in his usual pissed state would sing it right in front of a copper's face and before you knew it, he was in the back of a meat wagon quicker than Jimmy Saville exiting the morgue at Stoke Mandeville.

So, it was a bit of an 'acquired taste' type of establishment, no question, and not a place for a faint-hearted landlord. The pub still had its thatched coned roof from decades previously. It had three bars. The public bar housed a pool table and two dartboards. Fuck knows how no-one got a dart in the head.

It wasn't a big bar, and it was usually filled with boring fuckers who didn't do chat. (I'm always suspicious of anyone who goes into a pub just to play a game.) There was also the main bar, which had a raised area for karaoke or DJs at the weekend, and the back bar facing the car park. I usually flitted between the main and back bar. Funny how some people refused to sit in one or the other. Poor old Charlie Fingers died in the back bar. We all thought he was asleep as there was still Guinness left in his pint glass. It was only when one of the bar staff came to collect the pots and tried to wake him up that it became apparent, he was on his way to a drinker upstairs, bless him.

The arrival of Harry brought suspicion, as any new landlord does.

Even more so once he opened his mouth and the north-western accent popped out.

One of the blokes who spent his life in there, Geoff, shouted out once he heard Harry speak:
"Oh, for fack's sake! Not another fackin' northern cahhhnt!"
Probably not the welcome Harry was hoping for!

Harry was a diminutive bloke with Little Man Syndrome, add tight curly hair, a pocked face which gave his mush the complexion of a cheese grater, and a wardrobe full of Matalan clobber. His brief from the brewery was to clean the pub up. He brought a bird along to help him out, but she soon done the off when one of the regulars set light to the bar while she was serving another customer. For some reason, only known to the punter, he spilt lighter fluid over the wooden veneer and, in his incoherent state, dropped his fag into the flammable liquid.

The scream the barmaid let out as her sleeve caught fire, could be heard in Rayners Lane!

The locals showed their appreciation for the unexpected pyrotechnics, and, to a man, all started cheering. Once her arm was extinguished by a fraught Harry, everyone went back to their drunken conversations and carried on as though nothing had happened. The poor woman suffered the indignity of a nasty burn, a ruined blouse, being cheered at while alight, and then being hosed down by a right Toby.
Welcome to Northolt, love!

Harry was given some dough by the brewery and employed a couple of bouncers. He started flexing his muscles by banning all the 'characters'. My group of mates were mainly drinkers and grafters, so 'H' took a shine to us (or wanted us to snidely protect him during the week when the bouncers were off). He started laying on food for our Sunday team, Northolt Town, even though most of us thought he was a right cunt. He then told us he was going to come to training with us the following Tuesday. We couldn't really say no because, for a couple of our players, it was the only solid food they got all weekend.

Harry had already told all and sundry that he was on Stoke City's books when he was 16, so we were half-expecting a bit of a Micky Thomas or Jimmy Greenhoff type. Instead, we got Joey fucking Deacon. He was useless. 'H' couldn't trap a bag of sand and had the touch of a sex case.

One of the lads, Fozzy, would set him up for 50/50 tackles so someone like myself or Big Rich could go through him and leave the fucker crumpled up like a terylene shirt on Brunel University's Astroturf pitch. He'd come off hobbling at the end of the hour, still larging it though, undeterred.

"Fookin' hell! I've lost a bit of pace lads. There was a fookin' time I'd have run rings round you coons"

We'd roll our eyes and just hope he'd get in the car with Chapman and Iggy for a lift back to The Swan, just so we could keep all the boring bastards in one motor.

As time went on, the pub had less and less trade because he was banning nearly everyone. He even got one young fella removed for spilling his beer over a bird he fancied, hiding behind the bouncer as the amiable fella was launched out of the pub. Harry must have been getting heat from the brewery because the takings would have been well down. He asked me if I fancied doing a disco every Friday.

The conversation went like this:
"Could you fill the pub?"
"Fucking right I could, H. How much?"
"We charge the brewery 100 quid, so I'll give you 60"
"Fuck off, mate! It's got be at least 80 notes. I've got to hire the speakers"
"75 and it's a deal, you fookin' robbing Cockney bastard!"
"OK, but I'm not a Cockney, you northern mug!"
"Whatever! Just get it rammed. And don't tell anyone about our deal"

I was still bang into the house and its many offshoots, so mixing beats was my thing back then (or it would have been if I was any good. Me being 'in the mix' sounded more like pots and pans being thrown down the stairs, to be truthful). I'd finish off with a few old classics from the likes of Buzzcocks, The Small Faces, The Supremes and Bowie so it didn't go too full on.

In theory, it should have been an easy gig since this was my local, but anyone over 35 was moaning their bollocks off about listening to Shades of Rhythm or a De-Construction 12-inch. All the older mob wanted was shite like Phil Collins and Duran Duran and Harry was starting to wonder if he'd done the right thing hiring me. New people were coming in, but those used to a nicer gaff and more pleasant clientele never stayed all night.

One bank holiday, it all changed for Harry when he tried to pull one of the barmaids, who was my mate's wife. John was a placid, affable guy but when he found out, he got behind the jump and gave Harry a couple of digs. Even the lovable bouncer and main doorman, Micky P, was sick of him and didn't throw the fella out because he knew the twat was well in the wrong.

The next month, the pub was virtually empty. Harry had banned so many, we'd all had enough of the silly twat. We even stopped going in there after the Sunday games and headed for The Litten in Greenford instead. One Friday, after I'd played for three hours to an empty pub save for some old rotters off the Racecourse Estate. Harry told me the following Friday was his last night at The Swan. He also told me to "Keep it fookin' down, Stu, just in case some of my fookin' enemies come down". He certainly had a few of them.

Of course, I told everyone.

Friday arrived and I walked in to set up as per usual. The pub was half full at 7.30 with loads of old faces. Word had really got about. Harry liked a dip in the brewery's dough, so I could only surmise he'd nicked the money earmarked for the bouncers and skipped on their services for the night.

What a mistake!

By 9.30, the gaff was mobbed. There were blokes skinning up and having sword fights with pool cues in the public bar. People were dropping pills and a general air of anarchy filled the beer-drenched air. I was downing pint after pint, thanks to being looked after royally by old mates who had long been barred. By 10.30, I was proper hammered. Around this point, Harry was threatened with a kick round Northolt by a couple of heavies and was wildly gesticulating to me from behind the jump to turn the music off with the old 'slice-across-the-neck' gesture. I pretended not to see or hear him. Minutes later, 'H' came running over screaming.

"Stop after the next record! The Old Bill are on their way and some of your cockney bastard mates are going to get fookin' nicked, you coont!"

I didn't have a microphone, but I thought "Fuck it!'.

Fuelled by the gratis 8 pints of Fosters Export, I let the record fade out and shouted out to the pub.
"OLD BILL ARE COMING! NO RUNNERS!"

Everyone moody started hiding things and Gary moved his motor, which was full of lively Woolworths and Boots stock.

The Swan was now at fever pitch with agitated expectation for the Boys in Blue, so I dug out Sham 69's 'Hurry Up Harry'. Possibly the best-timed record I'd ever played, unless you were Harry, of course!

There were blokes on tables jumping up and down, flicking V signs at

Harry, and hanging off the jukebox by the side of the raised area where I was playing, laughing manically. Sally and Simone, in their scruffy cardigans, kept making the record jump by leaning over and demanding Wham's 'Everything She Wants', both pissed on the vodka they'd brought from home.

Richie came over and asks, "You got 'My Generation'? Go on! Put it on! The pub will go up!"

I was that hammered and getting off on the madness, I thought, "Too fucking right!"

As 'Hurry Up, Harry' was coming to an end, I caught Harry's eye. A mixture of fear and hate came over his face, which quickly turned to shock as another pint glass shattered on the floor tiles by the bar.

I couldn't find The Who in my box (probably a good thing), so I whacked on The Rolling Stones classic, 'Satisfaction'.

The sight of eight mates doing Mick Jagger impressions behind me as the Bill walked through the door is one that I'll carry forever. All putting out the big lips, elbows out, strutting about looking like a demented duck convention.

The first copper strolled in and just looked at everyone going absolutely Garrity in total dismay. Written all over his mush was "I wish I was at home".

He tells me in no uncertain terms, to turn the music off immediately, which I did once I could find the right button. A hush descended as eight or nine coppers walked through the doors and filled the front of the bar. There's a tension when suddenly from the back of the room, I hear my old mate, Grayzie, at the top of his vocal range - HARRY ROBERTS IS OUR FRIEND, IS OUR FRIEND ...

(Harry from Stoke was never seen again. Grayzie is still active in the Greenford area. The Swan shut down over 20 years ago and is now a small housing complex.)

In Bruges

The 1994/95 season brought European Football to Stamford Bridge for the first time in 23 years, due to our back-door entry into the European Cup Winners' Cup, when Manchester United beat us in the previous season's FA Cup Final to win the double, thanks to the bastard referee David Elleray (we won't count the other three goals). What a day that was, getting in the pub at 10am, meeting up with mates of old and hoping for the same result we'd already had twice that season, beating them home and away.

It was all going well until they got a penalty. The mood suddenly turned from pragmatic hope of a quick equaliser to pure hatred as Elleray, the pompous fuck of a ref, pointed to the spot for a second penalty. Even from where I was standing, at the opposite end of the ground, I could see, as did everyone else, that Frank Sinclair's typically clumsy challenge had been outside the box.

As Eric Cantona coolly slotted home past Dimitri Kharine, the United fans in our end were fully exposed, foolishly celebrating a second time, and brought unholy grief upon themselves. Blokes far milder than me were putting it on them and most were forced to leave with immediate effect. And those that stayed had the fun sucked right out of their landmark double-winning day.

It conspired that Captain Dennis Wise had collected many of the Chelsea player's spare tickets and sold them to a tout, with the dough going into the players pool, hence why there were quite a few United fans in our end. As the game progressed and the third, and then the final goal went in, all anybody was talking about was giving it to them outside even if it was pissing down.

We might have been at the start of a new era, but old habits die hard. No-one wanted to take the defeat graciously.

We should have qualified twice for the UEFA Cup back in the 1980s but the events of The European Cup Final between Juventus and Liverpool in 1985 put paid to that. An hour before kick-off, Liverpool supporters had charged at Juventus fans and breached a fence that was separating them from a neutral area. As the Italian club's fans ran to avoid the violence, a barrier wall collapsed and, tragically, 39 Juventus fans were crushed to death while 600 others were injured. The devastating loss of life meant that English clubs were banned from Europe for the next five seasons.

And, to add insult to injury, John Smith, the Liverpool chairman, disgustingly blamed Chelsea fans for starting the trouble rather than his own. No self-respecting Chelsea bod would have gone out there for that game.

After travelling to the games in the two previous rounds, in the Czech Republic and Austria, we were now at the quarter-final stage, but there were very few tickets available, as the Bruges ground only held about 20,000. Not that we gave a shit. Four of us drove over there in my trusty Vauxhall Cavalier.

The night before the game was typically mental. Standing in the middle of the main square, deciding which bar to go into, two fellow Chelsea bods came over and asked us what we'd done to their mate. We all looked at each other and wondered what he was on about. Next thing, one of them shouted to a couple of geezers some 20 yards back and, before we knew it, there were 12 or 14 fellas coming out of a bar with 'that' look on their face.

I turn round and one of my mates is away. Next thing, everyone's on their toes and we're being chased by a load of South London beer monsters. For the uninitiated, most fights at Chelsea games in Europe are usually with each other.

I mean, I'm no Seb Coe, but it wasn't long before I was away from these slags. Fred, who was a right fat bastard, got chased into a hotel but managed to avoid a hiding. We were well pissed off. Sounded like someone had got a whack after a day on the beer and the chisel, and it had bent a few of the older lad's heads who then went looking for revenge regardless of who hit their pal. Fred called me and I went and met him before making our way back to the hotel thinking "That's a bit out of order, all that"

The next day, we started drinking around midday and kept an eye open for scruffy older fuckers, the Belgian Special Forces - who we'd been told, were taking no prisoners and any locals wanting to throw firebombs at us. The Belgians love a pyro party. However, Chelsea's firm that day was fearsome, even more so than usual.

An hour before kick-off, rather than do the sensible thing and watch the game in a bar, me and Fred (having spent the last 7 hours lining our noses) decide to bunk in. The other (quieter) two had tickets in the Bruges end and knew how to keep schtum in such tight spots but us two, probably not.

As it happens, thanks to a zero tolerance on gate crashers, both of us ended up nicked anyway. The holding cell was directly under the home end so when they scored the only goal of the game, it felt like they were coming through the roof. By the time the match finished, there must have been 20 Chelsea in this makeshift nick, all in various degrees of fear, loathing and indignity. One bloke said that if we didn't make any noise, they might let us out.

Fred, of course, was the loudest, and he'd somehow managed to keep hold of his sniff. "SHUT UP, YOU SILLY CUNT!" he shouted, as he hoovered up another corner and then started banging on the cell doors for the 18th time. By this time, dehydration was starting to circulate round my body and the warm glow of the beer and ching was becoming a feeling of despondency and a wonder of what would happen next.

An hour after the game finished, we were taken to the ground's police station to be registered and then put on a coach. What we didn't know was that we were being filmed by news cameras as we boarded the bus. The media loved the 'Hooligan Abroad' story and it was much more than just us 20 causing issues. Fred and I would end up on *ITV News* for the next 24 hours.

The coach drove a short distance to a warehouse, and we were told to get off. The old wartime number of "This is where we get shot" did the rounds. As we entered the huge space, there were another 500 to 600 Chelsea fans already there! Not just your standard hooligans but many scarfers and shirt wearers too, including gentlemen in their sixties who certainly didn't deserve to be under lock and key.

A commotion at the back of the warehouse 30 minutes later made light relief of my irreversible hangover when some fellas managed to open a back door and escape. Eat your heart out, Cooler King! There was a canal outside and one of the lads decided to wade through it to safety. However, if he'd have looked to his left, he would have seen a footbridge 50 yards away that was now carrying 20 or 30 escapees!

The Belgian filth restored order as quickly as the doors had been forced open and the next couple of hours were spent waiting for the inevitable deportation. Then it dawned on me: my car was at the hotel with my keys in my room. I moaned like fuck to Fred about the strong possibility that we might not be allowed back into Belgium, and how was I going to get my car back?
Fred, tactful as ever, replied "SHUT UP YOU MOANY CUNT!"

As we were escorted for the final time onto another coach and taken to Ostend, we started thinking, "Well, at least we ain't been banged up over here and I haven't got to explain to my boss why I won't be back in work next week". Fred, being an independent trader, didn't have such issues to contend with.

The journey back on the ferry was a rough old ride. I must have thrown up three times but, to be fair, I could have been in a car or on a fucking magic carpet ride and it would have been the same. I'd swerved any type of food since breakfast some 20 hours earlier.

When we landed at Ramsgate, looking like Casual refugees, the press and cameras were out in force and the old Burberry scarf went up to cover the mush. One of my mates, Trevor, almost pushed a cameraman onto his arse as he palmed away his extended lens with some force.

The first thing we did was contact one of the lads we'd travelled out with to see if they'd been nicked as well. Luckily for us, they'd avoided a tug and said they would drive the car home.

Result!

Once we'd got to the safety of the train back into London, we both remarked on how it had all been a right craic and hoped we'd turn the game around in the second leg so we could do the away game in the semi-final, and what a result that we didn't get picked up by the cameras. If only we knew!

Chelsea did win the second leg 2-0 and went on to play Real Zaragoza. Unfortunately, we got proper turned over 3-0 by a Judas Poyet-inspired side in the first leg and there was trouble in the ground where I somehow managed to make the national news again for first giving it to the plod on the barrier, but also for running for dear life when they baton charged everyone back. I look like a right donut, to be honest. Again, I blame Fred for such uncharacteristic behaviour.

Chelsea did put on an impressive performance at home in the second leg and won 3-1 but went out 4-3 on aggregate, which brought an end to my European awayday specials for three years.

Some years later, over Christmas Dinner at Mum and Dad's in Clacton, my wife remarked on seeing me on television before we were together, not knowing my parents were unaware of the fun in Belgium. Trying to explain that one away with a mouth full of Brussel sprouts? Well, the irony wasn't lost!

Jocky Wilson Said

Primal Scream are a big part of the life I've led. They were very much a continuation of the seductive rock and roll myth that I read so much about with groups like The Stones and Led Zeppelin. From their 60s-inspired early singles, 'Imperial' and 'Velocity Girl' to the 90s rule-breaking classics such as 'Loaded' and 'Kowalski', I've been on that path alongside them, taking in the sights, sounds, hedonism, modernism, rock, roll, funk and soul that rules the head, heart and feet. They are just a fucking amazing band, especially live.

My first date with my wife Paula was a Scream all-nighter at Brixton Academy at the end of 1994. We got loved up and messed up. On the way out at 5am, in front of the waiting minicab drivers looking for their last decent earner of the night, my new bird tumbled down the stairs. I fell in love in an instant and tried not to laugh. A cut knee and bruised pride for her. A warm glow and dying embers of a pill or two for me.

There have been many Scream gigs over the years. The polka dot shirt 'Sonic Flower Groove' of ULU in 1987. Swing your pants. The cold, dismal and funereal 'Vanishing Point' tent shows in East London's Victoria Park in 1997, where a bloke in a wheelchair, completely off his tits, decided to spit on my Armani jeans. Glasgow's Barrowlands in April 1994, where we pushed the envelope so hard, we ended up in a flat in East Kilbride after, not actually knowing how we got there, where my car had gone or if the flat owners wanted to sleep with us or kill us. Or the night the Scream tore up Hammersmith Palais with the likes of Kylie Minogue, Michael Hutchence and half the caners in London in attendance.

Because we liked nothing more than getting on it to the Scream, the thought of going home after the band had gone higher than the sun, wasn't an option.

So, when a geezer told us about the after-show party at Turnmills near Farringdon, it was, as we say, a result. Especially being early hours on a Wednesday morning. After a quick drive across London, we make our way into the club and there's a fair few faces there. I end up in a conversation with Mark Gardiner from Ride, who were doing great things at that point. After a while of probably driving him mad, as I'd just banged half a pill, I join Rory and Fred at a table upstairs to calm me britches for a bit.

As we're all chatting pilled-up shit, I saw Kevin Rowland in the bar downstairs. We all love Kevin (who doesn't?) and started talking about the brilliance of Dexys Midnight Runners when it dawned on me that the enigmatic purveyor of the New Soul Vision looks like the *Viz* Comic character, Sid the Sexist.

The hair. The polo shirt. The profile.

I start to recite some of Sid's chat up lines to the lads. "I ain't got much pet, but it'll fill a pram" and "Do you like jewellery, love? Aye? Well, suck my cock 'cos it's a gem".

As the boys laugh, I look down and Kevin's staring at us. And he looks angry. Now the music's pumping at ear-shattering volume and there's no way he can hear anyone outside of his own space, but I start to get paranoid. Suddenly, everybody picks up on it and they start nervously looking elsewhere.

And he stares. And stares.

I thought, "Is he a master lip reader? Has he got special hearing powers? Has that last cheeky half sent me mental?". After the fourth time of looking down, he's finally turned away and is ordering a drink.

We all laugh again, wondering what had just happened. Is he from another planet? Super Kev! Spider Kev! The Six-Million Dollar Kev! More laughter and a quick check on the bar area to make sure he's not deciphering our conversation.

About half an hour later, I go for a slash and as I start to piss, Kev walks in. My blood runs cold. He doesn't look happy. One of the true musical icons is three traps down and I've mugged him off as a Geordie sex pest. He's not said anything, and he isn't looking at anything other than the wall in front of him.

I zip up, wash my hands and, as I walk past at speed in case he collars me in my semi-lairy toxic state, I just can't help myself.
"Why aye, Kev man!".

A gruff "Hello" and we both go about our business, me thinking I'm the funniest fucker in the gaff. Praise the lord I didn't see him in a dress.

Free (Like) Nelson Mandela

The 90s was my paradise. I really came into my own as someone who didn't give a shit about tomorrow and just lived for the moment, which was great for me, but not so good for everyone who cared about my wellbeing. I must have driven my mum and dad mental with my behaviour, and I'd just like to apologise now.

Sorry Mum. Sorry Dad.

Also, apologies to my girlfriend of the time, who I bought my first gaff with. I wasn't ready to settle down, even though I was 30. I just had a fire in me that wasn't going to be dimmed by anyone. Cocaine was everywhere, and me being me, I took to it like Harry from Stoke did to being a cunt. Chelsea were finally in the ascendancy and the football was double exciting to watch. And if it wasn't football, it was a gig. If it wasn't a gig, it was a club. Oasis, Primal Scream, The Verve and The Stone Roses were the perfect foil to get drunk and geared to. The million or so house, trip-hop, techno and other dance strands were for getting right on it too.

And I was getting the best terrace clobber through my Arsenal mate, so I was a man to know.

"You want something? Give me a shout"

"Stone Island jumper? What size?"

"Need some sniff? Nice bit of flake here, mate"

"Jack and Jills for the weekend? How many?"

I also had people who nicked stuff to order but, as in most clichés, the drugs took over. More money. More parties. More chaos. And I was fond of chaos.

I didn't sell shit gear and I was discreet. I drove a Vauxhall Cavalier and, apart from a nine-month period, I always had a day job to mask any sins (well, in my mind anyway).

Then I met a woman who turned it upside down while I was still with my then-girlfriend. She was saucy, dangerous and had issues, though she hid the last bit well for a while. Before I knew it, I'd gone full pelt into a relationship and split. I didn't stop to look back or take any responsibility for the hurt or damage caused, got paid out on my half of the flat, and booked a holiday for us to Jamaica.

Caution went out the window, and so did trying to contain a growing addiction to the powder and my new bird.

So off we went, January 1999, spending the dollar as quickly as I could and having it large. As we took our seats on the Montego Bay bound flight, there were about 12 travellers sitting three rows back. Now, I'm not one for stereotyping but someone from Gypsy stock is as recognisable as the Mona Lisa or Madonna. And often where there's a gypsy, there's Trouble. Yes, with a capital T. In the old days, the traveller usually spent their dough on their caravan or car. Clobber wasn't their forte. This mob were a new breed though, and it was the first time I'd been abroad with a travellers on a plane.

As the plane took off, there was a loud cheer from a few rows back and you could hear the duty free being slung down their necks. The flight was direct, and Heathrow to Kingston is a nine-hour schlep, so even an excited puppy like me knew that hitting the booze that early was a mistake. So, after 3 hours in, our friends were gaining the attention of the air stewards all too frequently.

"Oh, come on! We're on our holidays. Have one yourself, why don't ya!"
"Have you got any tonic boy?"
"What? We have to pay? Sheesh!" and so on.

With each passing half hour, the mixed group got louder and louder. On one trip to the toilet, I walked past the middle row to see one of the girls lying across three fellas singing Mousse T's 'Horny' shaking her fanny in a red-faced mush, pulling the sort of face in what can only be described as 'a lewd act, your honour'.

It wasn't my idea of titillation, I can tell thee.

Hour six, and tempers are fraying. Everyone up our end of the jumbo had seen and heard enough of the blatant disregard for airborne behaviour and there are kids being subjected to all sorts of language. Even for me, it ain't the done thing to shout out "Ya cunt, yas!" The stewardesses are struggling to keep them in check and a couple of the geezers are starting to get aggressive.

Then comes the catalyst.

One of the scumbags throws a drink and it hits this big lump sitting directly to the left of the mob. The homebound bloke takes umbrage and throws a couple of punches and it's all gone off. There's screaming and passengers in tears. I mean, a tear-up at 35,000 feet isn't for the faint-hearted, but somehow the stewardesses managed to calm the situation along with a couple of the cooler heads on board.

The captain tells us all we'll be landing at Norfolk International in the good old U.S. of A to remove the Diddys. Well, fuck me did that take the wind out of their sails. Sheepish doesn't come into it. A realisation for them that there's no escape and a sombre mood takes hold as many realise a further three hours have been added to the journey.
Cheers.

As the plane lands in Norfolk, everyone is told to remain seated while the local cavalry do their thing. As the NPD board the plane and make their way to the back where we're sitting, a massive cheer goes up, followed by a hearty round of applause. They're well equipped to deal with any of the party. It was like an episode of *TJ Hooker*. It was certainly a bit different from previous Old Bill interventions I'd seen on the old Inter City trains going to football.

As one of the horrible fuckers walked past, I gave him a cheerio and a wave.
The look back was priceless.

By the time we got to Montego Bay, we'd been travelling for around 17

139

hours, and we were both ready to hit the sack. We were only there for a week and had already lost a day and a bit, so we intended to make up for lost time by hitting the beach and bars.

After about the third or fourth day of trying to avoid sunburn, I called Lock to see how Chelsea had got on in a cup replay. Chelsea had won and I was about to hang up when he asked, "Oh, by the way. Was you on that plane with the Gypsies?" I said, "Yeah, how do you know about that?" "Oh, they've been on the news playing right up, saying they were innocent and only having a laugh"

I couldn't believe it. I gave Mark the full SP and said I'd see him next week at football. Next thing, one of our fellow passengers, who we encountered round the pool tells me *The Sun* rung his room looking for the story.

"I told 'em to fuck off! I'm on holiday!"

On our return to Britain, we were inundated with texts asking about the traveller mob. Turns out they were from a legal site in Lewisham, and it had caused internals amongst the dwellers who were all claiming benefit, and the attention on them was most unwelcome. A couple of days later, the international incident mob are on the *Six O'Clock News* having been let loose by the Yank plod. As they walked through the airport, being filmed and followed by reporters and camera crews like the Sex Pistols on manoeuvres, the bird who offered up her tush whilst lying across the geezers, excitedly shout to one of the news team, with imaginary handcuffs suddenly removed:

"LOOK! I'M FREE! FREE LIKE NELSON MANDELA!"
A traveller, on national and international telly, comparing herself to one of history's most gifted and honourable iconic figures?

Even I had to laugh at that!

Acknowledgements

I'd like to thank Chris Newson for his belief and push. Paul Miceli and Lucy Beevor getting this into a readable product. Mark Baxter for his kind words and constant inspiration. Tony Briggs and Wez for camerawork and laughter. My wife Paula for keeping it real. Ian Snowball for solid friendship and zen calm. Gary Crowley for enthusiasm. Steve Rowland for design. Simon Kortlang for being a top mate. Billy Sullivan for being Billy Sullivan. Greg Phillips, Mark Loughran, Georgia and Marcia Baillie for staying the course. All at Drum. The Saturday Club for continual entertainment and Joe Dwyer for radio shenanigans.

Previous books
Thick as Thieves – Personal Situations with The Jam, 2012
From Ronnie's to Ravers – Personal Situations with London Clubland, 2013
Supersonic – Personal Situations with Oasis, 2013
Soul Deep – Adventures with The Style Council, 2021